REACH OUT

REACH OUT
Evangelism for the Joy of It

Paul J. Foust
and
Richard G. Korthals

Publishing House
St. Louis

Unless otherwise indicated, the Scripture quotations in this publication are from the Revised Standard Version of the Bible, copyrighted 1946, 1952, ©1971, 1973 by the Division of Christian Education of the National Council of the Churches of Christ in the U.S.A., and used by permission.

Copyright © 1984 Concordia Publishing House
3558 S. Jefferson Avenue, St. Louis, MO 63118
Manufactured in the United States of America

All rights reserved. No part of this publication may be reproduced, stored in a retrieval system, or transmitted, in any form or by any means, electronic, mechanical, photocopying, recording, or otherwise without the prior written permission of Concordia Publishing House.

Library of Congress Cataloging in Publication Data

Foust, Paul J.
    Reach out.

    (Speaking the Gospel series)
    1. Evangelistic work. I. Korthals, Richard G.
II. Title. III. Series.
  BV3790.F67 1984   269'.2   83-27272
ISBN 0-570-03933-9 (pbk.)

1 2 3 4 5 6 7 8 9 10 IB 93 92 91 90 89 88 87 86 85 84

Contents

Preface			7
Chapter	1	My Father and I	9
Chapter	2	Evidence of His Hand Over Ours	13
Chapter	3	My Father as Senior Partner	18
Chapter	4	His Flawless Blueprint	22
Chapter	5	The Challenge of Enlisting Builders	29
Chapter	6	He Who Has Ears, Let Him Hear	39
Chapter	7	Basics of Building	45
Chapter	8	Cutting the Boards	54
Chapter	9	Nailing the Boards Together	61
Chapter	10	Applying the Paint	72
Chapter	11	Erecting the Birdhouse	86

Preface

How can individual Christians or, for that matter, entire congregations be motivated to execute the Great Commission that was given to us by our Lord? What will prompt them to discover new and exciting ways to carry out their ministry and to avail themselves of the many resources that will help them to accomplish the task placed before us?

Our primary motivation must always come as a result of the lonely trek to the foot of that cross which once stood on Calvary—a journey that each of us must make individually. There we observe God's Son, our Lord and Savior, suffering the agony of hell as the substitute—not only for each one of us individually but also for everyone who has been, or ever will be, born. Then, as we turn and go back to where we live and work, there must go with us the realization that God has placed in our hands the task of delivering this Good News to a world that is hungering for help. He, who could have selected the angels for this wonderful mission, instead relies on us frail and fallible human beings. We are His ambassadors; there are no others.

What can we do, having completed that journey, to inspire ourselves—and others within our church—to REACH OUT with loving arms and words to the open hearts and searching spirits of those who live around us? What can we say and do that can be used by the Holy Spirit to draw others to the waiting Savior? This book was written as an attempt to answer these two questions. It is the story of building God's Church, which is likened to building a birdhouse. It is an account of how the materials are first gathered and then put together in such a way that the resulting structure, "God's Birdhouse," becomes an inviting shelter for the "homeless birds" that inhabit our communities.

It is our prayer as co-authors that the Holy Spirit may use these words and thoughts, which we have struggled to bring to you, as a means for bringing joy and peace into your life. May He lengthen and strengthen your arms of love as you REACH OUT to those both inside and outside the church, and so may he help you to become better equipped to carry out the task of building "God's birdhouse."

Chapter 1

My Father and I

A friend of mine, Pastor Eugene Vetter, tells the fascinating story of "a boy and his birdhouse." It is a modern parable loaded with spiritual lessons that we shall unfold for you throughout the pages of this book.

A little boy comes dashing home from school, walks up to his father, and says "Hey, Dad, I've got a great idea. Let's build a birdhouse tonight just for the fun of it!" Dad says "Okay," and the project is on.

The little fellow drags a board out of the garage, but it is the wrong piece of wood for a birdhouse. But they are doing it for the fun of it, so they use his board. Dad plugs in the power saw. The boy turns on the switch and is about to push the board across the whirling blade when Dad calls, "Wait a minute. This is dangerous business. Let me help you!" He places his hand over the little boy's hand and proceeds to cut out the pieces of the birdhouse. The little fellow is in the way, so some of the pieces are not straight. If Dad wanted to build a perfect birdhouse, he would put the boy to bed and give it to him completed in the morning. *But that would destroy the joy of partnership!*

They proceed to nail it all together, and the lad emerges from the garage with two pails of paint. One is green and the other orange. Now, there is not a bird in the country that will live in a green and orange birdhouse! But they are doing it for the fun of it. They paint it green and orange!

That night the youngster can hardly sleep. He can hardly wait till morning. He is up bright and early and heads for school with his birdhouse. He is walking 10 feet tall!

When one of his schoolmates inquires, "Hey, where did you get that neat birdhouse?" he answers proudly, "My dad and I built it. We do things like this all the time—just for the fun of it!"

What a picture of a joyous partnership. In fact, what an illustration of the exciting partnership that every Christian has with our heavenly Father.

Our gracious God has chosen to draw a world of people back to Himself. This great assembly of redeemed and sanctified people not only constitutes the huge church of Jesus Christ, but each one also becomes a co-worker in expanding this "great birdhouse" of the church. We are not slaves driven by a self serving God but rather committed partners who cannot rest until the whole world of people is back with God, who made them, who loves them, and who has a plan for each to enjoy abundant and eternal life, which only He can give. My Father and I are doing great things together! We are building His "great birdhouse"!

Why God chose to select you and me to work with Him in this exciting project, we really don't know. We certainly do get in His way and contribute to many imperfections. If He wanted to build the perfect church, He would put us all to bed and build it Himself.

It is indeed dangerous business. His first 12 partners found it so dangerous, tradition suggests, that 11 of them died as martyrs. Yet with all the opposition of the devil and all his forces God has chosen to put His hand over ours, and it has turned out all right.

As the building of "God's great birdhouse" progresses, we are privileged to be filled with His Spirit and dedicated to His mission, so that our whole life becomes a series of "great ideas." My Father and I are doing great things together, all the time for the joy of it!

Those who are partners with God "all the time" have a suspicion that the reason why He does not put us to bed is that He wants us to enjoy this exciting partnership. When we pray "Our Father" and we add "Thy kingdom come," we are in earnest about the construction of "God's great birdhouse" of the church. The boards are not always right, the mission sometimes is dangerous, and our frail lives are often "in His way"; but He still chooses to work with us, He puts His hand over ours, and jubilantly proclaims, "I will build my church!" (Matt. 16:18).

A History of Great Ideas

Twenty centuries have passed since Jesus said, "Go ye," and countless thousands of builders have been incorporated into His mission. Each worker in the Kingdom has discovered that regenerate minds and lives can come up with great ideas that demonstrate fantastic ingenuity.

Great ideas have blossomed, from dreams into reality, as God's resourceful people moved the "Good News" from people to people, from culture to culture, from country to country, across oceans, mountains, and deserts. Christians have been willing to die to deliver the "one thing needful" to people the world over.

This great resourcefulness seems to spring from the conviction that Jesus Christ is the "one thing needful." During our earthly pilgrimage there are so many things that people in an affluent land like America consider necessary. What our forefathers longed for as luxuries, we now claim as necessities! These so-called necessities will some day become unimportant and we will then better understand that Jesus Christ has always been and will always be all-important!

Today we list our necessities as a house, a car, money, food, and clothing. Yet, eventually none of us will need any of these tentative treasures!

Some years ago when my oldest brother was unexpectedly moved from this life into heaven, I stood before his casket knowing that he would never drive his car again, that he would never live in his house again, that he would never spend a dollar again, that he would never eat food again, and that his one suit of clothes would rot! He needed only one treasure; he needed Jesus Christ, the "one thing needful!"

When Christians are convinced that Jesus is the "one thing needful," they cannot rest until God's love has been communicated to people who need to be loved, and God's Son becomes the Savior of people who need to be saved!

His Mission Is Not Triumphalism

There is an anti-Biblical message circulated among many that becoming a Christian will solve all earthly problems, turn our life into one big happy experience, and remove all pain and suffering. This is the message of triumphalism.

There are also those who leave the same impression regarding the experiences of committed ambassadors of Jesus Christ. Though optimism is a basic element of Christian faith, and though our Lord speaks of having life "abundantly," yet Scripture reminds us that we will have "many tribulations" and that "we are not contending against flesh or blood" but "against the powers, against the world rulers of this present darkness," which are much bigger and much more devastating than flesh and blood!

God's hand has always rested over those of all generations who were building His "great birdhouse" of the church—and they have each lived and served within His promise that "in everything God works for good with those who love Him," yet history has also demonstrated that He has not always guided His people around the troubles and treacheries of a demon-filled world, rather that He has led them through and they accomplished great things because His grace was sufficient.

Let no one conclude that those who are doing great things as coworkers with their heavenly Father will find this to be an easy path or that it will be devoid of disappointments and heartaches. We must through much tribulation enter the kingdom of heaven! In fact, Satan seems to throw special barriers across the path of those who pray and labor to make God's kingdom come.

There is indeed a great confidence that a child feels as he builds in the presence of his father. The father's hand over the son's hand guides the project along and is adequate to handle any barriers or disappointments.

Two thousand years of building is ample evidence that God can productively use those who "get in His way."

Furthermore, there are no problems before us that are bigger than God, who is beside us!

Chapter 2
Evidence of His Hand over Ours

We Christians usually don't think big enough when we consider that our Lord ascended to heaven, selected us as His instruments, and announced to the world "I will build My church!"

If we were born into and raised in a congregation of less than 200 members, that becomes our norm. Since most Protestant congregations number less than 200 members, it is normal for most of us to have a wrong concept of what our Lord means when He speaks of encompassing "all peoples, nations, and languages." We cannot quite conceive of a congregation that would involve thousands of worshipers, nor of a church that would reach into every country and teem with millions of believers in Jesus Christ, encompassing people from every segment of society.

When I was young, my mother, who is now in heaven, managed to get eight children ready for church, learned to drive an old 1924 Dodge, and took us seven miles to worship with a Christian congregation. My first remembrance of that little congregation was of some 35 members. They always seemed to be the same 35 people. I thought that was the whole church!

Expanding Our Concept

My concept of the size of the church grew immensely one Sunday afternoon when my mother loaded the eight of us into the Dodge to drive some 30 miles to a Lutheran Hour rally featuring Walter A. Maier, the famed radio preacher.

I saw parking lots jammed with cars, people coming from every direction, and a band playing "Stand Up for Jesus." We were part of a huge crowd that listened to a Gospel-saturated message that lasted over an hour. My immediate reaction was, "Wow, there are a lot more than 35 people who believe in Jesus as their Savior and Lord!"

Even with our much-improved communication systems, we Christians still need to have a more accurate concept of the size of the church. We tend to think that when those 12 disciples were expanded to 3,000 on Pentecost that was an abnormal operation. We need to know that the body of Christ is not a dwarf; it is a mighty giant.

If current statistics on the growth of the church are accurate, the Spirit of God is still providing great demonstrations of His power and performing impressive things. Growth figures tell us that over 60,000 people become Christians every day. Most of us who are committed to building "God's great birdhouse"—of the Church—are really impressed by this because we know that leading one person to the cross of Calvary often involves years of witnessing. We are also told by specialists in statistics that 1,400 new Christian congregations are established every week and that 85 million Americans gather for worship every Sunday morning. When we compare this with 5½ million sports enthusiasts who attend the three major sports events in any given week of the year, we begin to appreciate the size of "God's great birdhouse"—the church. There is no industry in the world as big as the Christian church; there is no country in the world that involves as many people as are involved in God's church!

It is, of course, true that no one on this side of eternity can compile accurate figures on the number of true believers. But if these figures are even half accurate, we ought to fall on our knees and thank God for the impressive operation of His Spirit in changing creatures to new creatures.

We are also well aware that the population of the world is expanding rapidly and that the Christian church is not keeping pace with the population explosion. But this only challenges those whom God has enlisted to build His "great birdhouse" to see that the fields are "white for harvest." Let this mighty army of witnesses march forward and reach out to a world teeming with people, *knowing that every one of them needs Jesus Christ.* The opportunities are enormous, because one half of the people who have lived in the entire history of the world are living today. What a time to build!

From Humble Beginnings

We are no small operation! Envision the first 12 disciples standing beside this gigantic 20th-century church of about a billion people! Knowing what those first 12 did to change the world, we must conclude that today God has much greater potential in His work force when He says, "I will build My church!"

The promise of His hand over ours seems almost academic until we begin the process of handling His Word and experience the operation of His Spirit changing lives. It seems that each Christian has to make this discovery before being convinced that God wants to use sinful human beings in His building program and that He does use them effectively, even though they "get in His way."

In the first organized parish that I served when I began my professional ministry there were only 38 adult members, and not all of these showed up when I delivered my first sermon.

I had been taught in the seminary that my labors in the Lord would not be in vain, so I proceeded to visit the unchurched homes in the community of 2,000 people. After planting the seed in their living rooms, I announced an instruction class to meet in my study (we had no church building), where we would further probe God's truths. That evening 18 came, and the study was too small for them. I solved the problem by lecturing between two rooms. It became apparent to me that His hand was over mine, I had a Senior Partner. That was a lesson I have not forgotten to this day. It is a lesson the whole church needs to learn.

Building with Sinful Human Lives

Today we are experiencing a movement in the church that involves lay people who are trained and deployed into their communities with a solid Gospel witness. These dedicated Christians have discovered a great fulfillment as they share what they believe and see others respond to their witness. They have also experienced the assurance that their Lord can use ordinary sinful humans by putting His hand over theirs and making it turn out all right.

We should not be surprised that 20th-century disciples are excited about the way God can use them. When Jesus sent out 70 to go "two by two, into every town and place where He Himself was about to come," we read of their response in Luke 10:17: "The seventy returned with joy saying, 'Lord, even the demons are subject to us in Your name!'" It is apparent that His hand was over them, and it is still over us!

Couple the experience of those first disciples with the identical experience of 20th-century Christians who are "off the platform" and out searching for and finding treasures, and you see a "Great Commission mentality." These are people who are convinced that His hand is over theirs. These are people who are full of great ideas and are teaming up with their Father to do great things together.

Because God puts His hand over ours, He is able to use us with all our glaring deficiencies! He can use people who are blind, deaf, physically handicapped, illiterate, very young or very old. God has no limitations! In fact, He can turn our liabilities into assets and use these to enhance our witness!

In an evangelism workshop I conducted many years ago there was a group of elderly ladies in the front row. I felt that there was little possibility that they would venture out into their communities and share the Good News. But I was convinced that their presence would be highly beneficial to their personal faith as they reviewed God's great plan for them. After all, they were living on the edge of eternity! In the course of the workshop every participant was challenged to "get off the platform and go search for treasures."

Five years later a young pastor asked me to speak at an evangelism banquet in honor of an elderly evangelism chairman who had led a group of visitors for five years. The chairman was one of those "front row ladies"!

She told how she had gone home and decided that she had been "sitting on the platform" too long. If she was going to get off, she had better move quickly! She also added that when she began her active witness life she discovered that God could use her in a wonderful way because she was so close to eternity and because she knew how precious those few remaining years were. She would witness to the world before she left it! God put His hand over hers! It was turning out all right!

In addition to all these impressive quantity results, which are so obvious wherever God's people are using the dynamic Word, we ought to be even more impressed by the quality results as we share in building "God's great birdhouse."

God puts His hand over ours, uses us to channel His Spirit into lives, and changes those who hate God into people who love Him, those who ignore God into people who serve Him faithfully, those who curse God into people who praise Him, those who hurt and destroy the lives of others into people who love and serve others, and those whose lives are a progressive death into people who live and enjoy eternal life. Indeed, He has His hand over ours and performs miracles through frail, sinful people like you and me!

Many feel like Peter when he was asked by our Lord to become "a fisher of men." Earlier in that story Peter said, "Depart from me for I am a sinful man, O Lord!" (Luke 5:8). But God used sinful Peter to speak the Word on Pentecost and be an instrument in God's hand in changing 3,000 people into new creatures. When He put His hand over Peter's it turned out all right!

Down through the centuries God has used no one except sinful human beings, and He has accomplished marvelous results.

Christians who sense their terrible inadequacy and sinful depravity need to recall that God's grace can wash sinners spotlessly clean, empower them with His Spirit, equip them with His dynamic Word, commission them as His ambassadors, and put His hand over theirs and use them as He has used forgiven sinners for 2,000 years to build His church.

Chapter 3
My Father as Senior Partner

It is significant that when the early disciples came to Jesus with the plea, "Lord, teach us to pray," He began His instruction by urging them to approach the throne of grace with that endearing phrase, "Our Father."

There is something assuring about coming to our Lord each day and remembering, right from the outset, that we have an intimate and secure relationship with Him. (It is like a little granddaughter who discovers the great love of grandpa for her! She really has got it made!) God's love for us is far, far bigger, and more productive than any human love. This Father of ours has put the whole universe together. He rules it day by day. He even designed and completed a plan by which we frail sinners could have absolute pardon and come back and live with Him as "our Father!" In fact, His will to have the whole world back with Him has become our will. We even beg Him to join us in our "great ideas" that honor His name and cause His kingdom to come to others! We are not building alone. We are doing great things together.

There are at least three Biblical truths that He has transmitted to us, with almost repetitious emphasis, in order that we might know for sure that "in the Lord your labor is not in vain" (1 Cor. 15:58). As we build, "God's great birdhouse" cannot fail. "The powers of death shall not prevail against it" (Matt. 16:18).

It is good for Christians to review these great truths in order to be assured of a viable ministry. How can it fail, since our Senior Partner is Lord of all? He designs no mistakes.

It almost seems tragic that less than two months after Jesus had given

His life for a world of sinners and rose again to prove Himself and demonstrate God's resurrective power, He ascended to heaven and placed the responsibility for delivering the Good News on those who had tasted His pardon, knew His love, and were enjoying His peace.

From our human perspective, it might have seemed better for Him to remain here and personally tell the world, "My peace I give to you!" (John 14:27).

But our Savior had assured His disciples "He who believes in Me will also *do the works that I do; and greater works* than these will he do" (John 14:12). This may sound like an exaggeration, until we see that because of His decentralization of ministry there are thousands of Christians reaching across every land, telling of God's love, forgiveness, and peace. Greater things are indeed being accomplished!

God designs perfect systems! This assures us that our witness life is a viable ministry. He designed it! Our Senior Partner provided the strategy for the fulfillment of His promise, "I will build My church!" I have solid evidence that His system is working, because it has reached all the way from Calvary down to my life! "He who believes in the Son of God has the testimony in Himself" (1 John 5:10).

This surely does not mean that Christians do not face disappointments in their witness life and discouragements as they labor to build "God's great birdhouse."

All of us have been turned away from homes where we desperately wanted to see the Good News received with joy; we have seen relatives continue in their unbelief in spite of our best efforts to share our faith; we have watched children reject the faith of their godly parents; and we have seen congregations shrink and die.

While it is not possible to read the mind of God and know why each of these disappointments should take place, we do know that His promises are sure. "My Word shall not return to Me empty" (Is. 55:11).

There are always human frailties in the church that impede the progress of God's mission. But there are impacts and seeds planted by the Word unseen by human eyes; there are children who come back to the Lord years later because they have something to come back to; there are timetables set by God that often seem unsatisfactory to us. If only we can trust our Senior Partner and know that His hand rests over ours, we can know that it will turn out all right!

His Tool Is Adequate—It's Dynamite

When the apostle Paul was sent by God into a world that had been hostile enough to crucify the Son of God and that would martyr 11 of His

12 disciples, he could still say, "I am not ashamed of the Gospel: it is the power of God for salvation." For "power" Paul uses the word *dunamis*, from which we get our word "dynamite." We could think of Paul as saying, "The Gospel is the dynamite of God!"

Our Lord has not only sent us into a world with some great news for every person—He even deposited in that news a special power that would change people's lives. It would cancel out their past depravity and change them into new creatures.

We are strangely motivated to share this message once we make the great discovery that the Gospel really is spiritual "dynamite." It changes lives from unbelief to faith, from old creatures to new, from servants of self to servants of God. It causes spiritually deaf people to hear; spiritually blind people to see; and spiritually dead people to live. The Spirit of God is present in this divine tool and performs miracles in people's lives!

This is one of the factors that encourage Christians! When they discover the dynamite of the Gospel, they are possessed by a determination to use it. There are men and women and children in every community who are stumbling through life not knowing where they came from, what they could and should be doing, and where they are going, and God has given us a tool to change all this. Jesus is the heart of this dynamic Gospel, and He says, "I am the Way, and the Truth, and the Life" (John 14:6). He promises us, "I am the Bread of life; he who comes to Me shall not hunger, and he who believes in Me shall never thirst" (John 6:35).

But dynamite does not go off by itself! This is why God in His great wisdom chooses to use His people to deliver His message of peace, pardon, and power.

Every Christian can point to at least one person who was a human link, just ahead of his life, who loved him enough and loved Jesus enough to bring the two together. Ahead of that person was another human link. If we could be in God's position and know what He knows, we would see those human links form a great chain that reaches from our life all the way back to Calvary!

What a sad and tragic thing it is to be the last link! We suspect that there are many Christians who have never shared their faith with even one person!

Those who know that God includes them in His system of delivering the Good News and who know the power of the Gospel are not about to be the last link. Part of the joy of their salvation is the privilege of sharing the dynamic Gospel and of watching it blast lives hardened against God and change the rubble into temples of the Holy Spirit and servants of Him who lived, died, and rose again for us.

These are the Christians who can say, "My Father and I are doing great things together all the time, just for the joy of it!"

His Divine Presence Is Sure

The disciples who stood on the Mount of Olives, watching Jesus fade from their sight, might have drawn the hasty conclusion that, at the very time of their life when they needed Him the most, He was abandoning them. The hostility of the world had reached an all-time high and the responsibility for the mission of the church had been committed to them. If we had been among that little band of disciples, our humanness would have insisted that the prospects for the future of the church looked pretty dim!

But when the disciples focused on God's promises (and His promises had always been kept), the picture changed completely!

"All authority in heaven and on earth has been given to Me" (Matt. 28:18). That meant He had the full ability to do as He willed any place! "Go...and make disciples of all nations" (Matt. 28:19). This imperative was given to every person who had stood beneath the cross and knew Christ as Savior and Lord. "Baptize and teach." These were the tools to build the "great birdhouse"—the church. Both were empowered with His Spirit; both were instruments designed by God to change lives, to wash them in the blood of the Lamb and to equip them for ministry to Him who lived, died, and arose again to make this all possible. Then came those crucial words of promise "I am with you always!"

No, He was not abandoning His people at a time when they had enormous need for His presence. He would be with them in their assignment; He would be with them in the baptizing; He would be with them in the teaching of His dynamic Word!

This promise is vital to the whole operation. No Christian is ever alone in the witness life! Christian Baptism is not an empty ceremony or ecclesiastical custom. Jesus Christ is present in an action designed by God to change lives. It is a "washing of regeneration and renewal in the Holy Spirit!" (Titus 3:5). The Gospel is not a benign doctrine; it is "the power of God for salvation" (Rom. 1:16). The Bible commentator Lenski says "What otherwise would be absolutely impossible now becomes gloriously possible." In a very special way, His hand is over ours with power to do the impossible. We are doing great things together!

How can this mission fail when He designed the strategy, He furnished the dynamic tool, and He even goes along. We are, indeed, coworkers with God!

My Father is doing great things through me!

Chapter 4
His Flawless Blueprint

Those of us who are partners in God's great plan—to reach out to a world of people who need to be reclaimed—must be familiar with His plan. We also must be convinced that it is not our plan but His! He designed it before we were around. He designed it in His grace; He drew the blueprint with His omniscience. It is flawless. God's plan is magnificent but it is also so simple that it works for all people in this great human mosaic of generations, cultures, and economic strata.

Our total awareness of and commitment to His plan is basic to our ministry of sharing it! We cannot share what we do not have!

In order to appreciate the whole scenario of God, we really need to envision the time in the world's history when there was a perfect partnership between God and man. Go back to Genesis 2 and observe the beautiful relationship in Eden between God and His first two human creatures. That was partnership at its best! But Genesis 3 explains why a plan of redemption became necessary.

There we see God's two junior partners hiding out in the bushes because they had betrayed Him. Their shame and fear separated them from the best friend they would ever have. The worst part of it was this, that their very nature had become depraved and dragged them down further every day. They never could come back by themselves to restore that desirable partnership. Worse yet, they would even pass this perverse nature on to their descendants and penalize every life from the very moment of its conception. If this sad and deplorable status was ever to be changed, man could not do it—it called for divine intervention, a plan of God!

A loving God who could make a magnificent universe was not about to see His foremost creatures forever separated from Him. His love and mercy compelled Him to provide a marvelous plan of grace that would be known the world over as the Good News.

The Old Testament Scriptures unfolded God's plan; the hills of Bethlehem presented it; the angel chorus sang about it; the New Testament Scriptures are saturated with it; the Son of God fulfilled it; the Holy Spirit communicates it; the Christian church confesses it; every Christian treasures it; and all the witnesses of Jesus Christ are sharing it!

The Great Transfer—Sin to Savior

Some suggest that God could have solved this dilemma in other ways. He could have wiped out those first two precious creatures (whom He still loved dearly) and started over again. This time He could have forced them to remain in the partnership and live in perfection. (This would have made them robots rather than free persons.)

Our wonderful God had a better plan! He would bring about the great transfer of all sin to the only One who could handle this devastating burden of the whole human race. His own Son would become the Savior of the world. "All we like sheep have gone astray; we have turned everyone to his own way; and the Lord has laid on Him the iniquity of us all" (Is. 53:6). God's own Son would become known to a world of sinful people as "the Prince of Peace." He would be indeed "a Prince." He would be the Son of a King; the King of the universe! He would bring peace to a people who by their personal depravity and actions were no longer worthy to be called "friends of God." This Great Redeemer would bring them forgiveness for a lifetime of waywardness; peace with God, who wanted them all back.

Dozens of Messianic prophecies of the Old Testament are God's message of redemption. They tell the great story of God's grace reaching out to a world of people created by God and now to be bought back by God. God would pay the life of His own Son, that the payment might be adequate. This would be the great transfer of sin to Savior. Thus the Christmas announcement, that personalized message, which still echoes throughout the world "To you is born a Savior!" This is the Good News!

The 33 years that followed were so urgent to the eternal well-being of every person on earth that our history books are all dated around this coming of God's Son. "Before Christ" and "after Christ" divide all the happenings of time. "With Christ" or "without Christ" divides all people!

He began His years of humiliation on this earth as a baby, He grew as we grow, He lived as we live—He was one of us. That's what "Emmanuel" means: God with us! But along with that true human nature, which was subject to the laws of God, was also His divine nature, which made it possible for Him to live perfectly by the law of God. He kept God's law to perfection for all humanity. "He committed no sin; no guile was found on His lips" (1 Peter 2:22). He was "born under the Law, to redeem those who were under the Law" (Gal. 4:4-5).

The human nature of God's Son also made it possible for Him to suffer for sin. He felt pain as any other human does! God's justice required that this be no mock payment. This had to be real. His divine nature added a second all-important dimension. He could suffer enough for the sins of all!

Much of the New Testament is devoted to God's account of the suffering and death of His Son. This was the heart of God's great plan. The transfer of sin to a Savior. We Christians are accustomed to spending 40 days of each Lenten season "watching with Jesus," meditating on His great love which prompted Him to pay so tremendous a price for our forgiveness. We have watched and we have heard Him say "It is finished!"

Three days later the whole plan ends in a grand finale with the resurrection. "Because I live, you will live also" (John 14:19). The false Christs died and rotted; but Jesus came back to life! This not only fulfills the Old Testament promise of God that the Messiah would not see corruption, and thus identifies Him as the Messiah, but it settles the whole question of resurrection and the doctrine of heaven. Now we can bear witness to a living Savior and to life that is eternal!

This Is the Good News!

The Great Transplant—Divine to Human Builders

One of the steps in God's great scenario that seemed so drastic that we might expect it to imperil His entire plan was the transplating of the mission from God's own Son to a small band of ordinary human beings. Could God really entrust this eternal worldwide mission to frail humans? Could this really be a flawless plan if human lives and lips were to carry it out?

He had the whole mission secured! He would place His hand over ours. It would turn out all right!

Only the Lord of heaven and earth with divine wisdom could design a plan to bring about such a major transplant. We humans watch with awe as we see Him do it with majestic simplicity.

He chose to deposit the power not in the person who is involved in His mission, but rather in the message. The message remains the same. It is as constant as the person of God and His gracious nature.

God's message of enduring love calls His wayward children back. It announces the transfer of the world's sin to a divine Savior. It is a message that is reinforced and empowered with the very operation of His Holy Spirit. It equips the frail humans whom He would disperse into all the world to build "God's great birdhouse"—the church!

This was all a part of God's strategy when He instructed those who would form the footings of the New Testament church to "stay in the city, until you are clothed with power from on high" (Luke 24:49). The Lord Jesus was equipping them and assuring them of adequacy, which He would supply, when He promised, "The Counselor, the Holy Spirit, whom the Father will send in My name, He will teach you all things" (John 14:26).

On the day of Pentecost those frail humans saw a powerful demonstration that the promises of Jesus were not empty! The Savior was no longer physically with them, but 3,000 were added to the church and the great building program was off to a flying start! It was apparent that the power was in the message; the Spirit of God was operating effectively! His hand was over theirs!

It was important that the disciples were convinced of the flawlessness of God's blueprint, but it was also urgent that their personal credibility be established. They were God's instruments to deliver a divine message. They needed credentials that would identify them.

Our all-knowing God had built at least three factors into this bridging process that provided impressive credentials. First, He brought about a miraculous change in the lives of His "new creatures," which caused the world to recognize the effectiveness of the Gospel. Second, by their willingness to suffer for Christ those disciples demonstrated to the world a level of commitment that could not be ignored. Third, He provided an overlap between Himself and them when they were given miracle-working powers.

God had provided well for the transplant of His mission from the divine to the human. In a very special way He had His hand over theirs.

Twenty centuries have passed since that time of transition. About a billion Christians in our world are ample proof of God's flawless plan. The power is still not in the men but in the message.

We may feel inadequate to be junior partners in building "God's great birdhouse"—the church. But remember that God used Peter, who once cursed and denied his Lord, at a time when Jesus had special need of a friend. God used Thomas, who doubted, even after the resurrection. God can use you and me. The power is not in the person but in the message.

The Great Transmission—Dynamic of the Holy Spirit

We Christians owe our very lives to God the Father, who created us, still sustains us, and provides us with all that we need for our physical lives. We owe Jesus Christ for our pardon which He bought with His life. He provided the only way back to God, who made us. But all this redemptive work of Jesus would never have reached our lives but for the work of the Holy Spirit. He communicated this message to us, who were spiritually deaf and couldn't hear it. He gave us, who were dead in trespasses and sins, a living faith, which embraces Jesus as our Savior. God reminds us that "no one can say 'Jesus is Lord' except by the Holy Spirit" (1 Cor. 12:3). Our very rebirth into God's great kingdom was an action of God's Holy Spirit, "That which is born of the Spirit is spirit" (John 3:6).

No wonder the Scriptures have such fantastic power to change lives. God Himself is present in them and is working through them. They have a divine dynamic that does things man cannot do. This is how "faith comes from what is heard, and what is heard comes by the preaching of Christ" (Rom. 10:17).

Not only does the Spirit of God transmit this message from Calvary to our hearts, He also takes over our hearts and becomes a force within us to change the nature and course of our lives. The Scriptures describe these changed lives as temples of the Holy Spirit (1 Cor. 6:19).

People who once ignored God now worship Him. People who once cursed God now praise Him. People who once hated and defied Him now love and serve Him. This is what Titus 3:5 refers to as "renewal in the Holy Spirit."

I have spent 38 years in the professional Christian ministry, and I have watched this dynamic of the Holy Spirit invading and changing lives. Christians begin to see things they never saw before, do things they never did before, endure things they never could have endured before, and live as they have never lived before.

Every Christian who lives in this world today (and there are about a billion of them) must give credit to the Third Person of the Trinity, who alone can transmit life to spiritually dead people, by faith hooking them up with Jesus, who came "that they may have life, and have it abundantly" (John 10:10).

No wonder witnesses for Jesus Christ are bold to proclaim God's Word. No wonder we go forth with great expectations into a militant world. We are well aware that God is present in the Word and changes lives. In fact, our own life is about the best and most convincing evidence we have that the divine dynamic is still working! His hand is over ours in a very personal way! The Holy Spirit is still the Great Transmitter!

It is right to give credit to the Spirit of God whenever a life is changed into a new creature. But it is also good to remember that whether we talk about the Holy Spirit or not, He is still working wherever the Word of God is applied to lives! The lesson that Christians need to learn is this: use the tool God gave us, knowing that the results are His business. We were sent to witness; He does the converting! This is a great partnership, my Father and I! He has not put us to bed; we are doing great things together, all the time!

The Great Transformation—Creatures to New Creatures

When our Lord in John 3:3 tells us that one must be "born anew," He is referring to the necessity of a great transformation in every life. All people, born into a world with depraved hearts (Ps. 51:5), inclination toward evil (James 1:15), and daily actions that betray their Creator (Rom. 3:23), need to be changed and given a new nature (Rom. 12:2).

Someone has compared this great transformation in our lives to the metamorphosis by which a caterpillar becomes a butterfly. Caterpillars are very restricted little creatures. They are limited in the places they go and the things they do. But the Great Creator designed a process in which they become a pupa in a cocoon and eventually hatch into a beautiful butterfly. This new creature loses its former limitations and begins to do things it never did before. It floats through the air with gracefulness and lives a completely new kind of life.

Christians who can remember the time before the great transformation in their life seem to appreciate this miracle of conversion more than those who were Christians from infancy. The former once felt entrapped in sin. No matter how they struggled, every day proved that they were slaves to sin. They could not free themselves. They crawled along the same old paths and did the same old things!

But our Lord performed a miracle in each of our lives when He brought us to faith. He took the pardon bought on Calvary and covered our life with Jesus' robe of righteousness. That not only canceled sins of the past, it gave us a new attitude toward sin for the future. Our repentant hearts began to fight sin and search for ways to please God. We no longer run from Him; we want to talk to Him in our prayers, listen to His message of love, and be guided by His gracious will. We know a beautiful freedom from sin, which we never knew before! We were transformed by God "from caterpillars to butterflies"—from old creatures to new!

While you may not be able to remember the days before the great transformation in your life, you can still envision what your life would have been without this miracle of God and what it is today because of the miracle. I have drawn a chart of my own life demonstrating these radical differences. I went to a different school because I am a Christian. (As an unbeliever, I never would have gone to a seminary.) I married a different wife because I am a Christian. (My wife, Ginny, would not have married an unbeliever.) I have 4 different children and 10 different grandchildren. I am in a different profession, I have different goals and purposes. I have different qualities and attitudes in my life. I spend my time and money in a different way. I have a whole different eternity before me! You see, God has transformed me into a new creature. My Father and I are doing things together instead of living apart. We are co-workers, helping others experience and enjoy this new life.

The Great Translation—Grace to Glory

Because our great God is a God of mercy, He has chosen not to leave us permanently in this earthly partnership. He promises that we will be here for "a little while."

When our Lord Jesus preceded us into heaven He said, "I go to prepare a place for you...I will come again and will take you to Myself, that where I am you may be also" (John 14:3).

When we read those beautiful descriptions of heaven in God's inspired Word and when we encounter many of the burdens of this sin-saturated world, we may be tempted to pray, "Come quickly, Lord Jesus!"

Admittedly, these are thoughts of Christians who seek rest from a weary life and comfort from a world torn with pain and heavy with burdens. Yet if God were to appear to us today and announce that our time here was limited to but a few days, most of us could think of many tasks yet unfinished and goals unfulfilled.

Who of us has completed our witness life and has no friends left to be brought back where they belong? We are still building "God's great birdhouse," and we need time.

It is a marvelous opportunity to share with the world before we leave it. Time is precious! We Christians are inclined to make better use of our time when we have an awareness that we live under grace. His hand of love is over ours every moment. "I can do all things in Him who strengthens me!" (Phil. 4:13). We may have many inadequacies, but there are no inadequacies in Him who is our Senior Partner! Time is spent productively when we labor with Him. "In the Lord your labor is not in vain" (1 Cor. 15:58).

There is urgency to our mission. Many parents have spent intense hours with sons or daughters who have wandered from the Lord, and begged them to come back before it is too late! Perhaps they have seen their earthly life already terribly penalized but know that it can still be salvaged! But there is another dimension of their life that is far more important. Someday it will be too late to salvage their life for heaven. God has so much to give them, yet they are throwing it away! Christian parents cannot rest until their children are back with God, who made them!

All this inspires us to search for more and greater ideas to work while it is day before the night comes (John 9:4). Eventually there comes the great translation from grace to glory. Let us witness to the world before we leave it!

Chapter 5

The Challenge of Enlisting Builders

Because all Christians should be committed to the joyous partnership and experience our Senior Partner's hand over ours, and because the Spirit of God opens eyes of faith to see and empowers us to communicate His flawless blueprint, we might expect that God's work force would be overloaded with volunteers. But congregations normally have not experienced this problem! With all these marvelous advantages, why are so few Christians discovering the joy and experiencing the fulfillment that the first 12 knew?

Perhaps the answer is not simple. The devil has his strategy going too! He has devised some rather effective obstacles. He is determined to keep the Good News from flowing from Calvary to the heart of all people, who desperately need a Savior. Christian witnesses need to examine some of the major obstacles and need to know that there are ways of overcoming them.

The Fear Complex

One of the most common strategies of Satan to block the flow of the Gospel is something that is as old as time and still just as effective as the day the devil introduced it! Fear always has been and always will be a problem for every Christian.

When our Lord Jesus was being tried, the night before His crucifixion, and a girl said to Peter "Aren't you one of His disciples?" big strong Simon Peter wilted and flew into a rage, eventually denying his Lord three times. How could the comment of a young maiden so completely unbalance a big strong fisherman like Simon Peter? Peter knew his Savior was in the hands of the enemies, and he wasn't about to be caught in the same trap. Fear had turned him from standing up for his Lord to denying Him.

Fear is the most common paralyzing obstacle to Christian witness. Train a group of Christians for a very simple neighborhood witness survey, requiring little more than asking some questions (which any youngster could ask) and watch grown men and women wilt when it is time to ring the doorbell.

Fear always has a paralyzing effect in other activities too! Place a 12-foot plank on the ground and ask a group of people to walk it from one end to the other and they will have no problem. Raise the same plank 50 feet in the air, put a ladder at each end, and ask the same people to walk it. Probably none of them can. They are frozen by fear.

There are at least three concerns that contribute to the fear that paralyzes our ability to witness: (1) Fear of getting hurt, (2) fear of failure to witness effectively, and (3) fear of penalizing some future witness. There are also some effective ways to overcome each of these concerns.

There was a time—and in some places there still is a time— when fear of getting hurt might be a legitimate expectation. In America today fear of getting physically hurt is probably not a valid concern. I have witnessed for my Lord in hundreds of homes and under a great variety of circumstances, and I can count on one hand the people who have been unkind to me. I have trained dozens of evangelism visitors and have found them returning greatly surprised at the positive reception that they experienced. If occasionally we do have a door slammed in our face, are we really being hurt? If the first disciples were willing to die for their Lord, has our commitment degenerated to the point where we are incapable of handling an occasional negative response? I know of only one way of overcoming this fear of getting hurt. Go out where the action is; give a solid but loving witness to Him who loves a whole world of people and watch your attitude change from fear to fulfillment! Our Senior Partner has ways of erasing fear when we actually get involved in His mission! Try it and make your own discovery!

We must indeed acknowledge that Christian witnesses do face the possibility of rejection, cynical accusations of being fanatics, and the mockery of those who feel threatened by the Christian message.

As long as we live in a world where Satan and his forces are in operation we should not expect to escape these experiences. Jesus said, "If the world hates you, know that it has hated Me before it hated you" (John 15:18). The two great plans of God and Satan are not compatible. One is bent on destroying; one on saving. We should not expect those who have never been regenerated to appreciate the abundant life and agree with those who have it.

In all the years of my witness life I have faced very little antagonism of this kind. And when I needed special assurance from my Senior Partner, it was always available in such great chapters of the Scriptures as Romans 8. Verse 18 says: "I consider that the sufferings of this present time are not worth comparing with the glory that is to be revealed to us." Verse 26: "Likewise the Spirit helps us in our weaknesses." Verse 28: "We know that in everything God works for good with those who love Him." Verse 31: "If God is for us, who is against us?" And Verse 37: "In all these things we are more than conquerors through Him who loved us."

The second honest concern that most Christians experience is fear of not being able to deliver an adequate witness. They simply feel inferior! This is completely understandable for those who are novice witnesses. The first time I stood at the plate with a baseball bat in my hands it was terrible! But the longer I stayed there and swung away, the more fun it became! And the first sermon I delivered before my classmates and a homiletics professor at the seminary was worse than the first ball game! But today I love to preach!

There is a sure solution to the problem of feeling inadequate. Practice will never make perfect as long as we are on this side of eternity, but it will develop competence and confidence! Some ordinary Christians have developed great competence in a very short time, once they went out where the action is! Our God-given talents and gifts do develop while they are being used. They do not develop while they are buried. This is why "in-service training" is so valuable! Ballplayers develop competence as they practice. Piano players develop confidence as they practice. Witnesses do too!

The third area of concern that I hear sincere Christians expressing is the fear that they might turn somebody off for a future witness or turn them negative to the invitations of the church or of other Christians. This is understandable. When we have had good relationships with people and we have reason to believe that an unwise remark on our part might ruin all the progress we have made, this is indeed reason for concern! That is precisely why our Lord urges us to be as "gentle as doves." Evangelists have often been guilty of more brass than empathy! Good relationships are very important if people are to hear what we are saying.

There is, however, a built-in quality, designed by God in the Christian life, that has a way of overcoming this third area of concern. It is that great quality of *agape* love. This is deep enduring love that God has. He loved people enough to go through His whole humiliation, suffering, and death because He wanted them back with Him where He could love them eternally.

When Christian witnesses are in God's mission with this love for people, it has a way of shining through. They are not out there as spiritual "headhunters." They just love people and are saying so with life and lips. This spirit of meekness and love communicates its own message. Such Christians do not mess up lives; they communicate with them, and their Senior Partner uses just such lives to build His "great birdhouse"—the church. He has not put us to bed because of our inadequacies; He leaves us up to enjoy our beautiful partnership.

The Clergy-Laity Dilemma

Since I have spent 38 years of my life as a clergyman and, originally, only 25 as a layman, I have a tendency to remember best the years of my professional ministry. These were all years when I felt a great compulsion to share my faith.

My attitude toward the professional portion has changed completely since that day in Seattle, Wash., when I knelt to take my ordination vow.

There was a time when I looked at my ministry as that of a "paid Christian." I was being paid by a congregation of Christians to lead the "pagan pool" in my community into a living relationship with Jesus Christ. In a city like Seattle this appeared to be a large assignment for one person to accomplish. But after a comparatively short ministry there I was moved by my Lord to a community of 2,000. Now the assignment seemed to be within reach!

I proceeded to announce to my little congregation, "You give me the names, and I will do the witnessing." This implied that they were not among those to whom Jesus spoke when He said, "You shall be My witnesses," and it certainly insinuated "You aren't capable of this, but I am!" In a small community it may be possible for a clergyman to live with this "paid Christian" philosophy and actually feel that, if God allows a normal life span, he can accomplish his ministerial goal.

But the Lord has a way of lifting and leading us in life to see broader horizons! He moved me to larger and larger "pagan pools," until finally I was in a community of 29,000 unbelievers within my immediate community. I did not have to possess any special insights to know that one "paid Christian" could not do it.

Those who have done some real probing of the Word have discovered not only that the message is all there, but also that there are some crucial basic guidelines that many of us have ignored and that provide the strategy to accomplish our assignment.

Every Christian a Witness

The first fundamental our Lord provided was that no Christian was left out of His building program. Jesus speaks to the whole church in Acts 1:8 and says, "You shall be My witnesses." He even designed the Christian life in such a way that we would all become "lights" to a dark world. He pleads with us to let our light shine before men. He provides His Holy Spirit to take up residence within us and become a constant influence on everything we say and do, lifting us to the kind of lives we live. God's people can be walking advertisements of what redeemed and sanctified people can become. The more God-pleasing our lives become, the easier it is for the world to see and know that Christ makes a difference. Because so many of God's people never rise to the level that God desires, the witness of the Christian church is blunted and the building of "God's great birdhouse" is impaired. When every Christian lives out the Christian life in conduct, worship, service, and in speaking up for his Lord, this all becomes a powerful witness to God, who made us, redeemed us, and lives within us!

It is vital that Christians are keenly aware that God does not leave us to our own devices to develop this kind of life. He urges you to drink deeply of the "pure spiritual milk, that by it you may grow up" (1 Peter 2:2). He invites you to the table of "His body and blood," to go forth with penitent hearts and "present your bodies as a living sacrifice" (Rom. 12:1). "We are His workmanship, created in Christ Jesus for good works" (Eph. 2:10). God has provided His people with ample sources of strength so that all of us may walk taller as His witnesses.

Some Are Evangelists

In His own marvelous strategy He has even chosen to equip some "specialists" to be available to conduct a ministry crucial to the building of His church. In Eph. 4:11 God makes reference to this group when He says, "Some [are] evangelists." In the same passages there are references to "specialists" in other areas of ministry, because God is concerned not only that the church should grow but also that it should function in many other areas of ministry.

Inasmuch as our concern at this point is with the building of the "birdhouse," we shall give our attention to the group of "specialists" that God refers to as "evangelists."

Christians who have read the parts of the Bible that speak of the church as the body of Christ, and thus are aware that Jesus is the Head and we the members, must have wondered at some time "what member am I?" Because each member has a special function, any practical person would naturally ask "What is my function? For what ministry did God design me?"

Many church workers have discovered by trial and error where they fit best in God's mission, but there should be some orderly way of making this discovery.

C. Peter Wagner, a Church Growth authority, has offered some suggestions that are a big improvement over the traditional trial-and-error system. He suggests that every Christian ought to begin by making a list of the gifts of God mentioned in the four passages that speak of the body of Christ (Rom. 12:4-8; 1 Cor. 12; Eph. 4:11-16; 1 Peter 4:10-11). From this list they should take a look at their personal life and try to select two or three areas of ministry that might seem to fit their makeup. Next they should experiment with these, looking for fulfillment, knowing that, if they have these special gifts for their ministry, they will perform well and thus will enjoy that particular ministry. Additional assurance comes from the affirmation they receive from other Christians. Finally, look for productivity, since God's gifts are not given for frivolous enjoyment nor personal glory but for the growth of the church (Eph. 4:12).

There is something very exciting about the enormous potential of the church when every Spirit-filled life is serving in the area of ministry for which God designed it. The whole team is on the field, and every member is playing the position for which he is best equipped.

There still are many "evangelists" who are completely unaware of their God-given gifts; many ministries are neglected by the church; much of "God's birdhouse" is unconstructed and unkept because God's gifts are not being discovered or not being used!

The Big Cop-out

The devil himself is the greatest enemy of the mission of the church. He takes great joy in persuading both laity and clergy to sidestep their ministry of building God's kingdom. Our sinful flesh jumps with glee if it can find some Biblical excuse for insisting that "evangelism is not my gift."

Laity and clergy often come to this conclusion before making an honest attempt to discover what their gift really is.

When there is this sidestep by lay people, they often assume that the ministry of witnessing has been erased from their life. They forfeit the marvelous privilege of partnership and choose to "go to bed" when they could be up, doing great things together with their Father.

When clergy are guilty of this cop-out, they sometimes assume that their congregation is automatically excused from the ministry of evangelism. There seems to be a false assumption that evangelism is optional. "Equippers of saints" sometimes operate as if lay people who were given the gift of evangelism need not be discovered, developed, and deployed.

Clergymen are enriched when they react to God's mandate to become "equippers of saints" for ministry. Pastors can spend their whole professional ministry serving as "paid Christians," doing what God wants the whole flock to be doing. But when their casket is closed those ministries are finished. Or they can heed God's call to become "equippers," and when they die their ministries continue through every saint they have equipped. God's system has a built-in follow-through! The style and (under the blessing of the Holy Spirit) the productivity of a clergyman depends on whether he operates as a "paid Christian" or an "equipper of saints."

While many of us have made this discovery very late in our ministry and have thus been deprived of much joy and productivity, God still had His hand over ours and we experienced many blessings because our Father uses us even when we get in His way.

This is not said to inject guilt into the lives of laity or clergy but comes from one who has too often been in God's way, who knows that we have an extremely gracious God, and who seeks constantly to find a better way to build "God's great birdhouse."

The Problem of Silence

A few days ago I stood before the open casket of my mother who had been moved by our gracious God from a rest home into heaven.

Mother was a faithful member of the church and was primarily instrumental for her eight children and my father all becoming Christians. Yet my mother was the silent type when it came to "speaking" the Gospel. I wish I could say that she often sat with us and spoke freely of God's love for us, of Jesus' death for us, and of our privileged life as temples of the Holy Spirit. Instead, my mother turned on the radio and gathered us around to listen to a great radio preacher; she loaded us into the car and drove us miles to church; when we moved far from home, she called the local preacher to check up on her wandering children. She just saw to it that the Gospel was wherever we were. Apparently she believed in the power of God's means of grace.

Yet, her life could have been even more productive had she learned to speak what she very much believed. If she had practiced this with all of us at home she would have been well qualified to speak the Good News to others outside our home.

My mother was so typical of many Christians that we must ask, "Why this silence?"

Perhaps this is partially explained by the fact that Christians are "strangers and pilgrims" in an alien world. We are not comfortable here. The ways of the world are far different from ours; the values of the world are the reverse of ours; the "truths" of the world declare the truths of God to be foolishness; the mores of the world contradict the moral standards of God. There is a natural tension between the wisdom of the world and the oracles of God. Sin has brought about a situation where those who walk in the Spirit have to be uncomfortable in a world where the flesh is dominant. What then is more natural than that we should withdraw from the pressure area and seek refuge within ourselves? Silence becomes the easier course! While this ought not be within the more comfortable confines of the Christian home, yet, especially in homes that are only 50% Christian, silence may become the price of peace.

In other homes there seems to be a tradition passed down from generation to generation that the expression of our faith is normally confined to a worship service. There is a strange separation of public worship and private living. Traditions are not easily changed, be they good or bad!

Christians have been trapped in this pattern of silence. Is there a way of breaking this barrier and moving into a completely new dimension of witness? Are there Christians who have made this breakthrough and discovered that if "silence is golden" then speaking the love of Jesus is far more precious than gold?

There are, indeed, thousands of God's people in our world who have made this great discovery, and they are living proof that it can be done! All of them went through experiences they once considered both risky and uncomfortable, but the breakthrough moved them into a new dimension of freedom.

There is a simple strategy, used by our Lord Himself, that people who search the Scriptures should never overlook. Jesus took His disciples with Him. Paul took Barnabas, Timothy, Titus, John, Mark, and Silas along with Him. The Teacher taught by doing and by demonstrating. He field-trained His disciples until the disciples had tasted the joy of witnessing.

Children do not learn to talk "overnight." The learning experience is a process that grows toward maturity. A noted scholar wrote a book entitled *How to Teach Your Child to Talk* and then followed it with a sequel entitled *How to Teach Your Child to Keep Quiet!*

Something similar to this has been experienced by many a Christian who was led by a brother or sister in the faith to venture forth into the witness life. They have discovered a new dimension of Christian witness that is so inviting that they must practice a great deal of restraint. They must be sensitive to the urgency of listening and discovering where people are before trying to lead them to where God wants them to be.

A backup strategy that has helped many Christians who would never consent to accompany trained evangelists on home visits is the process of initiating a witness experience between Christians. This can be done in the comfortable setting of a Bible class or an organizational meeting. It is nonthreatening to engage Christians in natural discussion of who was responsible for communicating the faith to them, what were the circumstances that brought them into contact with the Gospel, and what they believe in their relationship with Jesus Christ. This is precisely the nature of a witness. Once Christians start sharing with each other, the barrier has been broken and they discover that it is not beyond their ability to communicate the same message to others outside the church, in a less comfortable setting. There are, indeed, strategies available to help Christians deal with the nagging problem of silence.

Real Hard Work

One of the requests that every evangelism department hears from the church is: "Give us an easy strategy for evangelism; don't make it so complicated!"

Some church leaders have tried to provide 30-minute training sessions for their teams of evangelism workers, only to discover that they were ill-equipped for a very difficult assignment.

There is no easy way. Our Lord didn't commission us for a vacation; He called us to be *laborers* in the vineyard.

Evangelism is hard work. If congregations are afraid of hard work, then we have a serious problem.

Since our Lord has made us a part of the church militant as long as we are on this side of eternity and since "we are not contending against flesh and blood, but against the principalities, against the powers, against the world rulers of this present darkness," this is no easy assignment.

Hard work did not deter our Lord Jesus from going to Jerusalem and staying with His redemptive work until He could announce, "It is finished!"

It is to be hoped that none of us became Christians because we felt it was an easier way but rather because we were convinced by the Spirit of God that it is the only way that creatures can live in a proper relationship with their Creator. We do not serve our Lord because it is an easier way. We have presented our bodies "as a living sacrifice, holy and acceptable to God," which is our spiritual worship (Rom. 12:1). The very nature of our earthly existence is a journey with "thorns and thistles." Why should we expect that the most vital assignment our Lord has ever given us, the one He gave just before He ascended, should be easy?

Since we have been recruited into the army of God, we must be prepared to put on the whole armor of God and fight a good fight. Let's just assume that God is calling us to a difficult assignment—one that requires intense training and great commitment to His mission. Let's also assume that the joy that is ours when we see spiritual children born into the world will be great. The fulfillment that we experience in building "God's great birdhouse"—the church—will help us understand what Jesus meant when He said, "Take My yoke upon you, and learn from Me; for I am gentle and lowly in heart, and you will find rest for your souls. For My yoke is easy, and My burden is light" (Matt. 11:29-30).

Chapter 6

He Who Has Ears, Let Him Hear

Specialists in education tell us that one of the most difficult arts to teach is the art of listening. We often hear quips that "God gave us one mouth and two ears" but we have difficulty using them in this proportion.

Listening has also been a problem in the spiritual realm. God speaks, and the Scriptures become a best seller, yet two thirds of the world is stone-deaf to the Good News. The unregenerated simply are incapable of hearing until the Spirit of God gives them "ears to hear."

Even when about a billion people, because of the miracle of conversion, take their place beneath the cross and each confesses "He died for me," we still have a hearing problem when He commissions these same people to "go and tell!"

It is apparent that the whole church needs to practice the art of listening, and we need to beg the Holy Spirit to help us hear when God speaks.

After His ascension Jesus gave directions at least five times to spread the Good News of His death and resurrection for a world of sinners. The first 12 disciples had very sharp hearing, were loaded with "great ideas," and went forth with the firm conviction that His hand was over theirs! Let us listen!

Go Quickly and Tell (Matt. 28:7)

On that early Easter morning the few women who made their way to the tomb, expecting to find the lifeless body of their Lord, were greeted by an angel whose "appearance was like lightning, and his raiment white as snow," and they heard a messenger from God instruct them to "go quickly and tell His disciples." The Scriptures described their reaction as a mixture of "fear and joy." Nevertheless they went and delivered the message!

This was what we call today "inreach evangelism." They delivered the Good News to the church! When we within the church are firmly convinced that God's Son loved us enough to die for us and that He arose to prove that He was God's Son and the only Savior God ever sent—when we know that resurrection and the doctrine of eternal life has been demonstrated and is reaffirmed every Easter morning, then we have news to share that we cannot hide! "The love of Christ controls us" (2 Cor. 5:14).

The first postresurrection directive contains the whole message of evangelism!

"Go" implies that we Christians cannot remain in our own little sheltered environment and expect the Good News to reach the whole world. We are a "sent" people; our life is a mission; we are delivering a message of life and death.

"Quickly" implies that time is precious! When we stand by the casket of unbelieving friends, it is too late. When we read obituary columns, it is too late! When we stand crushed by the lifeless body of our unbelieving spouse, it is too late. There is a special urgency in our Lord's reminder, "Do you not say, 'There are yet four months, then comes the harvest'? I tell you, lift up your eyes, and see how the fields are already white for harvest" (John 4:35). Now is the time to harvest!

The third part of that early morning directive was "and tell." There is a tendency among many in the church to insist that we Christians only need to live out the Christian life so that others may see that our life is different and better, and then they will copy us and become Christians. While our conduct as God's faithful people is surely a vital part of the witness we bring to the world, yet spiritually dead people are incapable of copying. They need to hear the dynamic message that makes dead people alive unto God! Rom. 10:14 says, "How are they to believe in Him of whom they have never heard? And how are they to hear without a preacher? And how can men preach unless they are sent?"

It is urgent that we "go quickly and tell!"

Even So I Send You (John 20:21)

On the first Easter day the disciples were not convinced that their Lord had arisen; they were still living under the fear that they might suffer a fate similar to that of their crucified Lord. Therefore they met behind locked doors, where they found some measure of security.

The Lord Jesus knew that until they were convinced of His glorious resurrection they would never go forth to build His "great birdhouse"—the church. He would settle this problem by going directly where they were, allowing them to see His hands and side and then directing them "as the Father has sent Me, even so I send you!" (John 20:21).

Our Lord was saying to that nucleus of the New Testament church that locking themselves away from the world was the exact reverse of their divinely assigned mission. They were to unlock the doors and get out where people were who needed to hear that He who died for them had also risen! His message, "Peace be with you," capsulized the whole plan of God that was designed and carried out so that all sinners, at enmity with God, might come back and live at peace with their Maker. Sin had been paid for; forgiveness was fully procured; "His peace" was being held out to a whole world of people. This is the Good News!

Those early Christians unlocked the doors and moved out into pagan communities to knock on the locked doors of others who needed to be brought back where they belong.

The 20th-century church is still struggling with the initial fear complex of those early disciples. We are still more comfortable behind our stained-glass windows and closed doors, with people of our kind, than out in a world where we are strangers and pilgrims. But making our faith a private thing contradicts our Lord's Great Commission.

Congregations committed to ministering only to those within the fold and ignoring the far larger volume of people of their community need to hear our Lord's direction to unlock the doors and get out where the world is. We must listen more carefully when He says "As the Father has sent Me, even so I send you!'

Feed My Lambs...My Sheep (John 21:15-16)

The third appearance of Jesus to His disciples after His resurrection was another valuable evangelism lesson. An old pastor, now in heaven, once explained, "We need to sit down beside the text, watch it happen, and then tell people what we saw."

In John 21 we see the disciples having spent the night on the Sea of Tiberias with their nets down but catching nothing and then at His command moving the nets to the other side of the boat and catching more than they could handle. He was teaching them a great lesson as "fishers of men." We are frail and helpless in this great mission of our Lord, but He is perfectly able to fill the Gospel nets! When we go "fishing for men" we better not go alone! Plead with Him to go along and ask Him to fill the nets. And when He does, give Him the credit!

But Jesus had further business to attend to. He wanted to meet Peter face to face and give him a personal commission. After all, it was only a few days before when Peter had denied Him three times. Now our Lord wanted to use Peter to announce to the world that he did know Jesus, that he loved Jesus, and that he was willing to die for Him. Peter was a warning to Christians in his denial; now he became an example that God can use us no matter how low we have fallen. God can use us as surely and as mightily as He used Peter!

When Peter came splashing from the boat to the shore where Jesus stood, he heard his loving Savior say, "Peter do you *love* me?" In fact, Jesus repeated this three times, perhaps because Peter had three times spoken his shameful denial.

The first two times our resurrected Savior asked the question "Do you love me" He used the word *agape* for love—the intense love that God has for people. That's the love that wants everybody back, no matter how far they have wandered. Peter did answer yes, but he changed the word love to *phileo*, filial love. That's a much weaker love—the kind humans can have for each other. Even so Jesus indicated that He wanted to use Peter in His great mission. He said, "Feed My lambs." The second answer was the same. "Yes, I (filial) love You!" Jesus still would use Peter in His mission; He said, "Feed My sheep!" The third time Jesus even lowered the requirements; He asked Peter "do you (filial) love Me?" Peter was consistent. "Yes, I (filial) love You!" Jesus was also consistent as He directed Peter to "Feed My sheep."

What a dynamic message this speaks to the whole church! There are so many in the church who need to watch this text happen. They need to know that though they may have acted like Peter, and though their love may fall far short of the *agape* love of God, they are not in God's way, He does not put them to bed, He places His hand over theirs and says, "Lets work together and 'feed My lambs and My sheep.' "

You Shall Be My Witnesses (Acts 1:8)

Whenever an assignment is given to any of us, the first question that crosses our mind is, "How do I do it?" Consciously or unconsciously we begin to map out a strategy to reach our goal.

Our Lord knew that the assignment He was giving to His junior partners was a big one. It had worldwide dimensions. He knew that frail humans, who recognized their personal limitations, would shrink back. Had you or I been among that first band of 12 disciples and heard Him assign us to deliver a message to the whole world, we might well have responded, "Lord, You've got to be kidding!"

This is exactly why He began by saying, "You shall receive power when the Holy Spirit has come upon you" and then continued by giving them the strategy for their mission.

It is very easy to read a text like this and consider the promise of the presence and power of the Holy Spirit to be sort of academic, but the faithful Christians who actively share the Good News know that this promise is practical! No life has ever been changed from unbelief to faith except by God's Spirit. This is what gives such great confidence to every Christian witness. When the Third Person of the Trinity accompanies us, the power of God is in action. This makes the otherwise impossible completely possible!

The strategy is also practical. Jesus indicates that the disciples are to begin their witness in Jerusalem. Our witness life begins where we are, in our own homes, in our own communities. Relationships are important for witnessing. Witness is more than talking; it is living. The stronger our relationships, the better our opportunities to communicate the message. Statistics indicate that the most effective witness is by relatives and friends. Start in your Jerusalem!

Jesus told the disciples to move out from Jerusalem into Samaria. Crossing cultural barriers is not easy, but people who are different from us need Jesus Christ as much as we do. It would surely contradict God's whole plan of salvation if, after Jesus died for the entire world, we chose not to deliver the Good News to some people because they are different from us.

Our mission outreach is not optional. We must keep moving the Gospel from nation to nation, from people to people, until we have attained the goal of our Senior Partner—the whole world. This is a proper response to His strategy.

Listen to our Senior Partner as He places His hand over ours and says, "You shall receive power when the Holy Spirit has come upon you; and you shall be My witnesses in Jerusalem and in all Judea and Samaria and to the end of the earth! (Acts 1:8).

Go and Make Disciples (Matt. 28:19)

It would be impossible to write a book dealing with evangelism without referring to the Great Commission.

Sometimes I have envied the disciples who were privileged to walk with Jesus for three years. They heard messages from His lips that I would like to have heard and saw miracles I would like to have seen. They were present at Calvary, and they saw Him for 40 days after that victorious Easter morning. They saw Him ascend into heaven.

And yet, by a miracle of God I am a disciple! He Himself says so! "If you continue in My Word, you are truly My disciples, and you will know the truth, and the truth will make you free!" (John 8:31-32).

In fact, we have some advantages over those first 12. We can read His messages each day. They were put into print for us! We can relive the miracles as we read the inspired record. We can visit Calvary daily and never cease standing before the open tomb and the Mount of Ascension. In fact, we can walk with Him constantly and work with Him as His junior partners in building the "great birdhouse"—the church. We are His disciples!

This privilege He has not granted even to angels, to become disciples and be allowed to lead others into the same glorious relationship with our Lord. To make disciples is to transcend the humdrum of daily existence and to participate in a mission that is His and ours together—bringing lives back where they belong!

"Go make disciples" is the imperative of our Lord, directed to each of us who have been given "ears to hear." We have not been commissioned merely to lead people to the point where they are changed by the Spirit of God from unbelief to faith. We are commissioned to lead them beyond that point, using the same dynamic Word to nourish them into growing and functioning members of the body of Christ. It is the very nature of discipleship to be progressive. It is the will of God that we not only become justified and at peace with Him but that we become functioning disciples. "This is the will of God, your sanctification" (1 Thess. 4:3). The Great Commission begins with a universal Christian witness, continues with the life-changing action of God in conversion, and follows through with a life that glorifies God by worship, work, and witness. The Great Commission includes conversion but involves more than conversion. This is discipleship!

Chapter 7

The Basics of Building

The Scriptures are loaded with divine helps for the Christian's witness life. God gives his own blueprint of how we should live so that we will be a light to the world and salt to the earth, that others may see our good works and glorify our Father. God wants us to be living witnesses to Him every hour of the day. That's why He leaves us here in this vale of tears. We might think that it would be better for us if He moved us into heaven the minute we became Christians! But in 1 Peter 2:9 God reminds us that we were chosen to declare the wonderful deeds of Him who called us. If God were to move every Christian into heaven today, who would deliver the Good News to the nearly three billion people who still need to hear it? If we are not delivering the message, we are frustrating God's plan.

Though many of God's people have become sharper tools in His hands when they joined with other Christians and ministered to each other in evangelism programs, and though structured visits are great training grounds for the witness life, yet witness is not something we turn on Monday night and then turn off the rest of the week. If witness is an honest declaring, by word and deed, of the wonderful acts of God, then our participation in structured evangelism is a very small part of our total witness life. We are touching people all day long every day, and what we believe and what we are has to shine through. People around us surely ought to know whose side we are on, whom we love, whom we serve, and what great eternal truths are important to us.

If we are to carry out this purpose and become productive Christians who reveal God's great plan, there are some basic Bible truths that must be our firm convictions. These are divine truths that we affirm, that we will reflect in our daily living, and that we will boldly confess.

The Lostness of Man

Someone has said that many church members do not believe in the lostness of man. It is normal to hear the non-Christian talking about those who went to their "great reward" because of the noble accomplishments of their life. This really should not surprise us, since the "lostness of man" contradicts both the ideals of a humanistic world and of natural religion. Work-righteousness is normal in an unregenerate society. But what is disturbing is to hear church members speak as if a person could save himself by his own powers and accomplishments.

A great Bible doctrine that has never been popular with the world is the teaching of the total depravity of all human nature. We were all born sinful and inclined toward evil, we have rebellious natures, we think things that are offensive to God, and we say things and do things that are in conflict with His holy will. We are all sinners who get into more trouble every day. After living 63 years of this kind of life, how could I hope to stand before the holy God, who requires perfection? All Christians, if judged by their own accomplishments, are in trouble, for the Scriptures clearly say that "all have sinned and fall short of the glory of God" (Rom. 3:23).

The great apostle Paul, who remains one of the outstanding builders of the New Testament church, confessed that he was "chief of sinners." We who are the 20th-century builders are no different, nor are the people to whom we witness!

This is a doctrine crucial to our witness life. When unregenerate people are not convinced of their own lostness, they see no need for a forgiving Savior. If we are not convinced that a person without Christ is lost, we see no urgency to share with him the message of Calvary.

I have spoken to many persons about the time in their life when the only thing they will need is Jesus Christ and His priceless forgiveness, only to have them say "forgiveness for what?"

Christians who believe in the "lostness of man" will find this great Bible doctrine basic to communicating with people God's marvelous plan of forgiveness, peace, and life. In fact, it often has been said that the hardest part of evangelism is not getting people saved, but rather getting them to know that they are lost!

The Plan of God

We who are junior partners must clearly articulate, as we proclaim the Good News, that God's plan is built around forgiveness! Forgiveness is necessary if people are to come back to God, who made them. Forgiveness was at stake when Jesus went through His awful hours of abuse and suffering. Forgiveness was completely earned for all people when Jesus announced, "It is finished." Forgiveness was available to every person when He arose as the victorious Savior over sin, Satan, and hell. Forgiveness was to be delivered to a world of people who would get into more trouble every day and desperately need forgiveness. The Good News is that there is forgiveness, purchased by the Son of God, available to every life. When forgiveness is mine, I have peace with God, I am back where I belong, to live with Him and for Him. Those who are "washed...in the blood of the Lamb" become "new creatures" and begin to live not unto themselves but to Him who died for them and arose again.

Forgiveness is not something we deserve or earn or boast about. We can only boast of the love that God has for wretched sinners such as we!

Forgiveness is central to all the great doctrines of the church. The commandments underscore the universal need of forgiveness. The creeds focus on the life, death, and resurrection of Jesus Christ to bring forgiveness to the world. The doctrine of Baptism proclaims: Be baptized for the forgiveness of sins (Acts 2:38). The Lord's Prayer guides us before the throne of grace to plead "Forgive us our debts" (Matt. 6:12). The Lord's Supper takes us back to Calvary and invites the church to drink of "My blood, which is poured out for many for the forgiveness of sins" (Matt. 26:28). Oh, the joy of those who can say with David, "Thou didst forgive the guilt of my sin" (Ps. 32:5).

The Christian witness must say to the unregenerate that there is a way to come back. This way is never earned by man; this way was earned by Jesus Christ, who holds out to wayward sinners His forgiveness as He announces "My peace I give to you" (John 14:27). This is the very thing that makes our salvation sure. Forgiveness was not earned by us. It was earned by God's Son!

God's Limitless Love

Those who deny the total depravity of man often attempt to discover some good in human nature that would result in God selecting certain people for forgiveness.

The Scriptures do not base God's plan on anything in man. They base God's plan squarely on the limitless love of God. They point us to God, who loves all people and who would spare no sacrifice to redeem all people, who "like sheep have gone astray" (Is. 53:6).

There are countless illustrations of human love that resulted in people giving their lives to save the life of others who were dear to them. There are even some who sacrificed themselves for persons who were unknown to them.

There was, for example, a man who plunged into any icy river to recover a child and then returned a second time to rescue the child's mother, but he lost his life in the second attempt. Apparently the man had never met the people he sought to save. The child will tell, the rest of his life, of that heroic display of courage to which he is indebted; the mother will never know the sacrifice that was made for her!

The limitless love of God is infinitely greater than this. God loves people who have never loved Him and never will! Jesus could even say of those who nailed Him to the cross, "Father forgive them!"

The Scriptures remind us that it is no major accomplishment to love those who love us and do good to us, but the challenge of the Christian life is to love our enemies. God's love has always reached out to His enemies! Those who remain enemies of God for years, those who reject His gracious invitations repeatedly—to these rebellious enemies God sends His people to invite them to come and be washed in the blood of the Lamb! God's limitless love pleads with a world of sinners to come back and taste and know that God is good! God's great plan is not based on our goodness; it is based on God's goodness!

The limitless love of God provided a flawless plan; the limitless love of God proclaimed a golden thread of Messianic promises; the limitless love of God was incarnate in His own Son, who lived the perfect life for us; the limitless love of God went to the cross and endured the tortures of hell in our place; the limitless love of God sends out a great host of witnesses of His love; the limitless love of God calls back a world of people whom He made, whom He loves, and of whom He desires that not one should be lost. Oh, come and "taste and see that the Lord is good!" (Ps. 34:8).

Those who are conscripted into God's great army of witnesses have experienced God's love and are constrained by the love of Christ to proclaim to every life they touch, by word and deed, "God loves you—no matter how far you have wandered." They know also that His loving hand is over theirs as they go about His mission. The limitless love of God is their message, and it compels them in their mission.

Evidence and Action of God's Love in Baptism

Christianity is always only one generation away from extinction, since each succeeding generation must experience the miracle of conversion. But our all-wise God has not left the conservation and perpetuation of His mission to chance. He has designed a marvelous system by which parents, who have a God-given love for their children, just naturally want the best for them.

Parents are aware that children are not only a great blessing, who normally add happiness to their homes, but they also involve parental responsibility. This is especially true during the early years, when parents are privileged to shape a developing generation. Parents become responsible for the nutritional, emotional, medical, educational, and spiritual needs of every life God places into their home. When parents falter, the developing generation is penalized.

Parents who have accumulated a vast store of the physical things of life are determined to provide their children with the same abundance. Those who are spiritually rich find it very natural to communicate this to their offspring.

During the Old Testament, God initiated the spiritual transfer by requiring that all of the male children be entered into a lifelong relationship with Him by a system He Himself ordained in the covenant of circumcision. God spoke to Abraham, who bore the title of "father of the Old Testament believers," and ordered: "This is My covenant, which you shall keep, between Me and you and your descendants after you: Every male among you shall be circumcised. You shall be circumcised in the flesh of your foreskins, and it shall be a sign of the covenant between Me and you" (Gen. 17:10-11). Lest parents become negligent and allow the years to slip by, He even required that it take place on the eighth day of the child's life. "He that is eight days old among you shall be circumcised" (Gen. 17:12). They were to begin their life with God, spend their life with Him, and live their eternity with Him. The act of circumcision was a very human action that was assigned not to the child, but to the parent. When parents were negligent, the child was penalized. This requirement of parental responsibility was God's way of bridging the spiritual gap from one generation to the next.

Circumcision was much more than a cutting of the foreskin. This was a God-ordained action that brought children at the age of eight days into the family of God. God said, "So shall My covenant be in your flesh an everlasting covenant" (Gen. 17:13). God's plan of forgiveness through the coming Messiah was applied to this new life. He who would bear the sins of the whole world became their Savior and "though [their] sins are like scarlet, they shall be as white as snow" (Is. 1:18). Conversion was as much of a miraculous act of God in the Old Testament as it is today.

But inasmuch as circumcision pointed ahead and attached their lives to the awaited Savior and to the shedding of His blood, it was only natural that circumcision would no longer be necessary when the promise was fulfilled. The Savior came and died for a world of sinners. They were no longer awaiting the birth of a baby nor the shedding of His blood. No longer would God point ahead; now He would point back to His completed redemption and transmit forgiveness from the cross to individual lives.

Our Lord Jesus instituted the new covenant of Baptism, by which God signaled a new era. Baptism became God's action by which lives would be brought into a living relationship with Jesus. "As many of you as were baptized into Christ have put on Christ" (Gal. 3:27). This would be much more than a religious ritual, a cultural custom, or even a Christian symbol. It would replace God's old covenant with a new one, bringing lives into that same relationship with Jesus Christ. It would be, according to God's own description, "washing of regeneration and renewal in the Holy Spirit" (Titus 3:5).

Parents who want the best for their children should see Christian Baptism not as just a fine Christian custom, but rather as a claiming of the promise of God, in which God effects a miracle. By God's action, His love moves into a life in a "washing of regeneration." No human merit is involved in this action. This is an action of God's grace. Those who fully accept the great Bible doctrine of grace will find this miraculous action consistent with God's plan described in Ephesians 2:8-9: "By grace you have been saved through faith; and this is not your own doing, it is the gift of God—not because of works, lest any man should boast."

No other doctrine in Scripture is more relevant to the perpetuation of the Gospel from one generation to the next than this divinely ordained New Testament covenant, bringing lives to share a new relationship with Jesus Christ, incorporating them into a new kind of fellowship with God and with one another. They become members of the body of Christ. This is evangelism at its best as part of the responsibility of every Christian parent.

As we build "God's great birdhouse"—the church—we who are privileged to be Christian parents would do well to pray daily that God give us the commitment not only to enter our children into this eternal covenant but also to assume the responsibility of helping them grow in grace, nurturing them in the Word, as they drink "the pure spiritual milk, that by it [they] may grow up to salvation" (1 Peter 2:2). The goal of Christian parents is not only spiritual birth but also spiritual growth into mature discipleship.

Builders to Reach Every Creature

When our heavenly Father designed His church, He was not satisfied merely to make godly parents responsible for communicating the Good News to their children, nor even with turning every child of God into a walking advertisement of the Good News; He even handpicked and especially equipped some "evangelists" to reach out into the segments of His creation where there is need of a more intense heralding of the Good News. He supplied all of these with adequacy for the mission by giving each one His Holy Spirit. God became active in people and thus provided a divine dimension of power! These Spirit-filled people equipped with the dynamite of the Gospel became His workers. His arrangements were thorough and sufficient to carry out His mission. "I will build My church!"

Christian congregations that are blessed with leadership with a Great Commission mentality will challenge every parent to treasure Christian Baptism and nourish every reborn child of God into a life of mature discipleship. They will lead their family of faith daily to draw divine strength from the Word and become real beacons of the Gospel. They will discover, develop, and deploy those God-provided evangelists to reach into every corner of the mission field of their community.

When these three overlapping units of builders are possessed by the will of God, "not wishing that any should perish," knowing that His hand is over theirs, and realizing that they are the only builders God has, then God's mission is alive and well!

These are people who know that they have access to the work of God in evangelism, access to the power of God in His Word, and access to the heart of God in their prayers to invoke the presence and blessings of their Senior Partner.

Prayers That Produce

Some theologians have pointed out that faith accomplishes great things not because of what it is—but rather because of what it has a hold of. Faith that grasps a false god can be devastating! Faith that grasps Jesus Christ is eternally beneficial.

This is also true of prayer. Prayer is effective, not because it is some kind of meritorious act. It is effective because it grasps the promises of God. The possibilities of prayer are as big as God, who promised His children, "Ask, and it will be given you; seek and you will find; knock, and it will be opened to you" (Matt. 7:7).

Christians who are convinced that God has left them in this vale of tears, after they became Christians, in order that they might be the "salt of the earth" and the "light of the world" (Matt. 5:13-14) will find their prayers a glorious opportunity to bring their Senior Partner into their witness ministry. Daily prayer for those who do not know of God's forgiveness reaches out to power beyond our frail lives and invokes the blessings of God. "The prayer of a righteous man has great power" (James 5:16).

Many parents are separated from their children by hundreds of miles or sometimes live in the same house and yet are separated by invisible barriers but have begged God daily for a miracle of conversion in these precious lives and have discovered that He can do the seemingly impossible.

The concept "your God is too small" is true of all of us! We simply cannot comprehend the ability of the Almighty. No problem is too big for Him to handle! God is not offended if we "bother Him" daily with the burden of some soul who is dear to us and dear to Him. "Pray constantly" (1 Thess. 5:17).

But what seems inconsistent is when Christians are willing to pray *for* but not willing to speak *to* those for whom we feel a spiritual burden. God has given us the tool of His dynamic Word, which changes lives from unbelief to faith. "We cannot but speak of what we have seen and heard" (Acts 4:20). We reach up to the throne of God in our daily prayers, and He has promised to hear us! He reaches down into the lives of spiritually blind people with His Gospel and gives them sight to see what they could not previously see, faith to believe what they could not previously know, and a life to live on a level they could not previously enjoy.

Christians who pray for and deliver the Good News to lives that are precious to us and to our Lord will discover that our Senior Partner has His hand over ours!

Relationships That Last

The Christian life involves relationships. There was a beautiful relationship between God and His first two creatures in the garden. Relationships were destroyed when sin built a wall between God and man. Relationships were restored when God's Son paid the price for the forgiveness of sins and thus brought reconciliation between God and man. Relationships are built as each sinner is washed in the blood of Jesus Christ and brought into a spiritual relationship with all members of the family of faith. These relationships are strong and lasting!

The oneness that Christians experience with each other is stronger than the tie that binds blood relatives together. We are one in the Spirit! I have a greater closeness with my brothers and sisters in the faith than I have with blood relatives who have no faith!

This is the new relationship that develops when wayward people come back to God, who made and loves them. They become our new brothers and sisters in the great family of God. Before this, they were set on a course of death. God said: "The soul that sins shall die" (Ezek. 18:4). Now they are set on a course of life that includes eternal life! This is the relationship that lasts!

Lest we develop a false security and assume that Christians cannot fall from the faith, we should recall the once faithful but later "foolish Galatians" of whom St. Paul said, "You are severed from Christ, you who would be justified by the Law" (Gal. 5:4). And in Hebrews 6:4-6 we read of those who had "become partakers of the Holy Spirit" and had "tasted the goodness of the Word of God," yet had committed apostasy and crucified the Son of God.

Indeed the Lord has provided strength to resist the threats of the devil and all his forces. He begs us Christians: "Brethren, be the more zealous to confirm your call and election, for if you do this you will never fall" (2 Peter 1:10). In 1 John 2:24 we read "Let what you heard from the beginning abide in you.... Then you will abide in the Son and in the Father."

We have great comfort when we know that this family relationship can last eternally. We look forward to the day when beautiful reunions will take place in heaven, where parents and children will no more be separated.

This relationship will become its best when brothers and sisters in the family of faith will gather "before the throne of God, and serve Him day and night in His temple; and He who sits upon the throne will shelter them with His presence. They shall hunger no more, neither thirst any more; the sun shall not strike them, nor any scorching heat. For the Lamb in the midst of the throne will be their Shepherd, and He will guide them to springs of living water; and God will wipe away every tear from their eyes" (Rev. 7:15-17).

Born to Grow Up

If we Christians are to reach this glorious goal and are to function in the years yet before us as junior partners in building "God's great birdhouse"—the church—we must be nurtured by the Word to "grow in grace and knowledge of our Lord and Savior Jesus Christ" (2 Peter 3:18).

Babies are not born into the world to remain babies! They were born to grow up!

Christians are reborn into the kingdom of God not to remain spiritual babies. We were born to grow up into the mature discipleship life! It is truly exciting to see a spiritual baby born into this eternal kingdom. Those who have seen this happen have watched a miracle take place! However, it is even more exciting to watch these lives grow and mature into functioning, lively disciples who can say with St. Paul "For me to live is Christ" (Phil. 1:21) and "It is no longer I who live, but Christ who lives in me; and the life I now live in the flesh I live by faith in the Son of God, who loved me and gave Himself for me" (Gal. 2:20). This is a life of one who can say with confidence, "My Father and I are doing great things together, all the time—just for the joy of it!"

Chapter 8
Cutting the Boards

A little boy came home from school one day and, running up to his father, said in an excited voice, "Dad, I have a great idea. I would like to build a birdhouse this evening. Would you have the time to help me?" The father took one look at that eager upturned face and knew that he could not refuse that request. "Of course, son," he replied, "it would be fun to work together to build one. Why don't you look in the garage and see if there are any boards that we might use for this project."

The boy did as he was told and had soon gathered a collection of boards of various sizes and shapes. But as he was completing his task he heard someone call his name. Looking up, he saw a group of his neighborhood friends, all carrying gloves, balls, and bats, heading for the nearby ballfield. Responding to their shout of invitation, he dropped what he was doing, picked up his own glove, and ran after them.

He returned much later, exhausted from a strenuous evening of play. Completely removed from his mind was his desire to build a birdhouse with his dad. The eager anticipation once experienced had long since vanished. Even a gentle query from his father was insufficient to bring it back to mind.

In the meantime, the boards that the boy had gathered lay partially hidden at the side of the garage. Soon the ravages of nature became apparent. One board became warped and twisted, and another showed signs of decay. A man, walking past the garage one day, picked up one of the boards and used it as a temporary brace. Not one ever became part of a birdhouse, in spite of the dreams and plans that once existed in the mind of the little boy.

This example may sound absurd to you. After all, what boy would run off and forget all about a project that he had been planning with his father? Yet it does happen more often than we would like to admit, not only in the world of boards, nails, and baseball—but also in the spiritual counterpart encountered in building "God's birdhouse."

The previous chapters of this book dealt primarily with the gathering of the material, accomplished by bringing the Gospel message to those who do not as yet know Christ as their Savior. This is what we commonly call "evangelism." Unfortunately this often becomes the end rather than the means to an end, as far as our efforts are concerned. We, like the little boy, often lose interest in the project at that point. Why does this happen?

I have often thought about this, for I have been guilty of that very thing. Several factors might account for our actions, with particular circumstances determining which, if any, apply. The first pertains to the excitement of the initial contact versus the long haul. The second is related to the kind of evangelism program that is being conducted. The third may result because of a misinterpretation of the Great Commission.

Who hasn't observed a child start on some project, tackle the initial phases with great gusto, and then just as quickly lose interest and go on to something else? And who hasn't gone through that same kind of experience time after time? Many projects were started with high resolve and interest, but today they lie only partially finished. It requires determination to stick with something or someone until the final result is achieved, particularly if the task becomes long, demanding, and repetitive. Yet that is exactly what God asks us to do. He wants us to go beyond the initial excitement of sharing the Gospel message with strangers—of bringing them to church and introducing them to the pastor. He also asks us, as His people, to stick with them for the long haul.

Sometimes we lose sight of this if we are using a Kennedy-type program, where heavy emphasis is placed on the training of team members. It is very easy to become so involved in the teaching requirements that the true purpose of the call assumes a secondary role. I know, because it happened to me, and the resulting pangs of conscience are still present.

In 1971 I was asked to serve as a visiting lay evangelist in our District. The task meant assignment to a congregation for a 4-month period with the sole purpose of training lay people as evangelists, using the method outlined by Dr. James Kennedy in his book *Evangelism Explosion*. Ten teams had to be taken out on visits every week, with heavy emphasis on exposure to different types of situations. The latter was felt to be necessary because their first participation in the presentation came during the seventh week of training, and all were supposed to be qualified trainers upon the completion of 16 visits.

In spite of the pressures of training, the Lord worked through the Gospel message and touched a number of hearts. On more than one occasion we were present as someone was, in the words of Jesus, born again. The memory of the excitement and thrill of those moments still lingers with me. Afterward we, figuratively speaking, would take this spiritual baby in our arms and carry it out to the car. I would then drive up to the church entrance. There we would all get out and carefully place this helpless infant in front of the church door. Any feeble cries of protest were met by our words of reassurance, for we were quite certain that someone would be coming by shortly to take care of the feeding and diaper changing. Then we drove off with hardly a backward glance, searching for other spiritual babies waiting to be born.

That arrangement might have worked, had we made certain that there were members of that congregation who were trained to "check the doorstep" every morning. Unfortunately, that was not the case. We were so intent on conducting a good training program that the problem of caring for the newly born was neglected. Since then I have often wondered about the number of those abandoned infants that may have starved to death because nobody was there to feed them—how many perished from the ravages of neglect because there was no one to carry them inside.

It might be well for us to again read—and study and contemplate—the Great Commission given us by our Lord in Matt. 28:19-20: "Go therefore and make disciples of all nations, baptizing them in the name of the Father and of the Son and of the Holy Spirit, teaching them to observe everything that I have commanded you." Notice in particular two things. First, His command is to make disciples, not converts. Second, the instructions are to baptize and teach; it is not either/or—it is both/and.

How easy it is to emphasize one in favor of the other. Our task might become more apparent if we were to substitute learner for the word disciple, for that is what it really means as it is used in the Greek. All Christians are disciples, for you become one at the moment of conversion. We differ, one from the other, only in that we are at various stages of growth. Some are infants and a few have reached maturity, but most of us fall somewhere in between. But no matter what step we are on in our upward movement, we still are—and will always be—learners. Because of that our spiritual growth should be a continuous process, and our need for assistance in that growth is unending.

That is why the task the Lord leaves with us is that of acting as both herald and shepherd. He wants to use us as His instruments in both conversion and sanctification. To accomplish that mission requires a broad range of skills and abilities, and it is here that we encounter the problem of cutting the "boards" to proper "size." Permit me to explain.

One of the marks of a great teacher is the ability to use illustrations from everyday life to aid in understanding difficult subject matter. Jesus did that, and His description of the conversion of a sinner in terms of being "born again" is a prime example. How much easier it becomes if we envision that mysterious spiritual process in terms of the birth and growth of the physical child, and therein find our own particular role.

The birth of the physical child usually calls for the presence of someone skilled in assisting the mother during the delivery. At one time that individual might have been a midwife. Today in all probability it will be an obstetrician, an individual equipped and trained to handle that task. But once the birth takes place, this person steps aside and a new group takes over. There will be nurses in the maternity ward, parents to take the infant home, people who will provide food and clothing, teachers to assist in the education of the growing child—and many more who in one way or another play a part in helping this child grow to maturity.

Pause for a moment and think of the multitude of people who played a part in your own "growing up." Think of those who loved you and made you feel wanted, who provided for your physical needs, who shaped your life and ideas through their teaching, who worked and struggled with you through thick and thin. Think of the wide variety of talents, training, and skills that all of this required. What sad shape you would be in today if the world were populated solely by obstetricians, or teachers, or even parents. It required the cooperation of many to make your maturity a physical reality.

Just so it is in our spiritual birth and growth. The efforts of many gifted individuals must be brought into play if that spiritual child is to survive and grow to adulthood. We need the "spiritual obstetrician," the evangelist, to go out into the community with the Gospel message and through that means to be used by the Holy Spirit to assist in the spiritual birth of those still waiting in darkness. But at the same time we also require the skills of the "nurses," "foster parents," "teachers," "suppliers," and the like—all working in close cooperation to meet the needs of that one who has, in the words of Jesus, been "born again."

Now do you see why we need boards of different sizes and shapes if we are to build "God's birdhouse" so that it will be structurally sound? And can you imagine how impatient God must feel at times as He, with His hand over ours, watches—and permits—us in our sincere but often misguided efforts to "shape the boards" that have been gathered? Let me give you several examples of where we sometimes go astray.

We often act as though the entire "birdhouse" can be built from boards that are all cut to the same dimensions. Suppose, for example, that we sponsor an evangelism Sunday. The speaker is a gifted evangelist with a true zeal for the souls of the lost. During the sermon the impression is given that everyone in the congregation should display that same ability and desire—and that this is the sole mission of the church. In other words, everybody should become an "obstetrician" if they want to serve the Lord.

That may not have been the message that the speaker wanted to convey, but that is what it was perceived to be by those in attendance. What resulted were feelings of guilt, frustration, and lack of worth. Those "boards" cut out of a different pattern were left with the impression that they were of the wrong size and shape and therefore would be of little use in building "God's birdhouse." Those same feelings could also be generated during a service stressing the merits of teaching in the Sunday school, or extolling the virtues of spontaneous giving. Maybe it has even happened to you!

There are other times when we assume that an individual's occupation is an automatic determinant of the "shape" of that "board." For instance, the new member who teaches in the community elementary school or high school is welcomed with open arms and immediately relegated to the role of Sunday school teacher. The teller from the local bank becomes the treasurer, those skilled in construction are nominated as trustees, while the mothers and fathers with the most children find themselves serving as members on the board for education. In each of these cases little regard may have been given to the gifts or desires of that particular individual—and sometimes those "boards" just do not fit as we think they should. That, too, may have happened to you!

It almost sounds as if we are in need of a blueprint, doesn't it? Fortunately, that is just what God, in His wisdom, has provided for us. It can be found in the source to which we should always turn when we encounter difficulties of this nature—His Word. St. Paul provides the most vivid description of various "boards" in that "birdhouse" we are struggling to build—only he does it in terms of parts of the human body.

Hear what he says in 1 Cor. 12:12-20: "Just as the body is one and has many members, and all the members of the body, though many, are one body, so it is with Christ. For by one Spirit we were all baptized into one body—Jews or Greeks, slaves or free— and all were made to drink of one Spirit.

"For the body does not consist of one member but of many. If the foot should say, 'Because I am not a hand, I do not belong to the body,' that would not make it any less a part of the body. And if the ear should say, 'Because I am not an eye, I do not belong to the body,' that would not make it any less a part of the body. If the whole body were an eye, where would be the hearing? If the whole body were an ear, where would be the sense of smell? But as it is, God arranged the organs in the body, each of them, as He chose. If all were a single organ, where would the body be? As it is, there are many parts, yet one body."

How easy it is now to substitute *birdhouse* for *body*—and the size and shape of the individual boards for the eye, ear, hand, or foot. Variety is surely required. Yet all are needed—and all are of equal importance—if "God's birdhouse" is to be both structurally sound and physically attractive. But one problem remains, namely, what are these boards to look like? Where is the pattern that should be followed?

Again it is God who comes to the rescue, and again it is St. Paul who is used to provide the answer. It is found in the three letters in which he discusses spiritual gifts: Romans, 1 Corinthians, and Ephesians.

The subject of spiritual gifts is often either avoided or ignored, primarily because it has at times been the source of controversy and/or confusion. In some instances that happens because individuals overemphasize a few of the gifts in comparison with the others, thereby creating a class of "super Christians." In other cases it takes place as we try to sort through that list of nearly 30 attributes, trying to find the area of service that is designed for us.

My confusion ended when I read a book that explained this complex subject in such a way that it made sense and at the same time was Biblical. The book, entitled *Journey into Usefulness*, was written by James Mahoney (Nashville, Broadman Press, 1976). His contention is that there are only seven spiritual gifts, or enablements. The others are what he describes as either "executions" or "effects."

The key Bible passage is 1 Cor. 12:4-6. Here St. Paul says: "There are varieties of gifts, but the same Spirit; and there are varieties of service, but the same Lord; and there are varieties of working, but it is the same God who inspires them all in every one." Notice that he speaks about three different things—"gifts," "service," and "working."

Rom. 12:6 is a most important passage on this subject: "Having gifts that differ according to the grace given to us..." There follows a listing of seven of these gifts—strictly speaking, the only such list in the Bible. In 1 Cor. 12:28 we are told: "God has appointed in the church first apostles, second prophets..." There is a similar list in Ephesians 4:11. These are areas of service, ways in which a gift can be used in the church. Finally, in the last section dealing with this subject matter, 1 Cor. 12:7-8, we read; "To each is given the manifestation of the Spirit for the common good. To one is given through the Spirit the utterance of wisdom, and to another the utterance of knowledge...." The gift being put to use in an area of service can result in a message that the Holy Spirit can use to produce different kinds of "workings," or effects, within the hearers.

Rom. 12:6-8 gives us the blueprint that shows us the shape of the boards that are brought together to form "God's birdhouse." There we read: "Having gifts that differ according to the grace given to us, let us use them: if prophecy, in proportion to our faith; if service, in our serving; he who teaches, in his teaching; he who exhorts, in his exhortation; he who contributes, in liberality; he who gives aid, with zeal; he who does acts of mercy, with cheerfulness."

Seven different gifts—seven unique boards, each shaped individually, handcrafted by God for us to use as we work together to build that "birdhouse." Here is that list: (1) prophecy (which, by the way, means forthtelling or explaining, not foretelling the future), (2) serving, (3) teaching, (4) encouraging, (5) giving, (6) leadership (as the New International Version has it), and (7) showing mercy. Not an imposing list, is it. Would you have thought that something as commonplace as serving, or giving, or encouraging, or even showing mercy, could be a gift? And yet how like God to use such "boards" to build His "birdhouse." Nothing fancy or pretentious in the eyes of the world, but how vital, how necessary, how beautiful when we look at that structure through His eyes.

One of those pieces describes you, as they also describe every other Christian. Why can we be so certain? Because God has told us so! In 1 Peter 4:10 we read: "As *each has received a gift*, employ it for one another, as good stewards of God's varied grace." You have received a gift. There is no need to struggle—and search—and feel envious of others. Every Christian has been uniquely endowed so that, by being gathered together, the body is formed—the "birdhouse" can be built.

Here is a building that is one-of-a-kind. Anyone with a tiny bit of skill and knowledge, a few tools, and the necessary boards can put together a reasonable structure that will serve as a nesting place for birds. Such is not the case, however, when we approach this task. Here the boards are more than slabs hewn from felled trees—they are living human beings. That is why it requires a blueprint from God—it takes His hand over ours, tools are needed that only He can devise and provide—if the building is to become a reality. Again, it is He who provides us with a picture of the finished product, one that differs only in the building material used. We read in 1 Peter 2:4-5: "Come to Him, to that living stone, rejected by men but in God's sight chosen and precious; and like living stones be yourselves built into a spiritual house, to be a holy priesthood, to offer spiritual sacrifices acceptable to God through Jesus Christ."

God has provided the boards and indicated the shapes. Now is the time for us, with His hand over ours, to start putting it all together.

Chapter 9
Nailing the Boards Together

A little boy and his father were busy building a birdhouse. The boy had gathered some boards and, though some were slightly warped and others were rough, the father agreed that they were usable. The two worked together, cutting them into the proper shape, with the large hand of the father gently guiding and protecting the small hand of his offspring. Consequently a feeling of pride began to well up in the son, even though not all the cuts were perfect.

When the time came to pound in the nails that would hold it all together, the young lad insisted that he could do it all by himself, even though the heavy hammer was almost more than he could handle. The father stepped back and watched as one nail after the other was either bent or came out at the side of the board. His offers of assistance were met by vocal objection so he stood to one side and patiently continued to observe. Finally a few of the nails were so placed as to hold the pieces somewhat together, and gradually the unstable shape of a birdhouse began to emerge.

The next morning the boy went to school and happily told everyone about the project that he and his father had completed the previous evening, and how the birdhouse was now hanging in their yard, awaiting occupants. That evening a storm arose, and gusts of wind shook the newly completed structure. Several of the loosely nailed boards separated from the others and fell to the ground. Gaping holes were left in the tiny home, rendering it unsightly and almost useless as a songbird's bungalow. To this day is has failed to attract the wanted inhabitants.

Does the story sound familiar? It should, because it happens often in the task of building "God's birdhouse." The evangelism team has gathered the materials and the tentative shape of the "board" has been identified, all of which is followed by attempts to somehow fasten the new member onto the structure of the church. Then something happens—the newcomer disappears—and we have another statistic known as a "backdoor loss." For some reason or other the well-intentioned nails were either bent or missed the mark. They just did not hold.

What went wrong, and what can be done to prevent it? How we long to know the complete solutions to those problems! We have developed programs and ideas for retrieving those who have wandered through the backdoor and have left the premises—and a number of these have been relatively effective. There are also some "birdhouse builders" who station themselves at the backdoor and there try to persuade those who are about to leave to remain inside. In essence they are acting as a repair crew, trying with whatever methods are available to reattach the board that has become dislodged. These also have their moments of success.

But the best position by far for preventing the loss through the backdoor is to stand at the front door and begin working with the newcomer at that point. What this amounts to is using additional nails, and maybe even some glue, to strengthen the attachment of boards that were loosely fastened in the initial effort. This is a relatively easy task when we are working with wood, hammer, nails, and a real birdhouse. It is quite another matter when the subject is a human being with all the diverse needs, desires, and characteristics that are encapsulated in that person. Where do we begin to approach a problem as complex as this?

It might be good to start by trying to determine the needs of the individual, inner yearnings that created a desire—or amenability—to being gathered up as a potential part of God's birdhouse. By this I am not saying that the faith in Christ as Savior was self-generated. The creating and instilling of faith is still *solely* and *completely* the work of the Holy Spirit. The tools He uses are always the same—the two means of grace— Baptism and that precious Word, the Gospel.

But this is not to say that there was no preparatory work. Jesus explains that rather clearly in the parable of the sower (Matt. 13:1-23). Only some of the seed that was scattered fell on good soil and there produced a crop. That good soil is the result of careful, and often long, preparation and cultivation. It may have been rocky to begin with, requiring the hammerblows of adversity or the chilling frost of loneliness as a pulverizing agent. Or it could have become packed and hard from long exposure to the measured tread and hot glare of those who walked over the newly formed marl, never stopping or showing concern for what was beneath their feet.

It lay there, crusty and impervious to all that fell upon it—until the gentle words, "I care for you" touched that patch and penetrated that which had felt a thousand pounding heels.

These are the kinds of inner needs that often serve to prepare the soil for the sowing of the seed—and consequently there exists in many new Christians the ardent hope that these needs will be met through the experiences now being encountered. This places an added responsibility on the shoulders of the "birdhouse builders," that of identifying not only the shape of the board but also the nature of the inner longings that are present. Discovering just what these deep desires are will help us determine what kinds of "nails" or "glue" will work best in order to securely fasten the "board" to the "birdhouse."

Sociologists and psychologists have spent untold hours in studies and interviews, trying to determine the nature of the deficiencies in life that cause people to seek the comfort of the religious community. Pages upon pages have been written to describe their findings. Unfortunately, most of us do not have ready access to these studies and might not be able to interpret them if we could. But that does not excuse inaction on our part, for we still have a source of information that is close at hand. In fact, it lies within each of us. What we must do is examine our own inner feelings in light of the question, "What are the kinds of needs that I have, and which of these are uniquely satisfied by the church to which I belong?"

Just why do you belong to a church—and what do you find there that is not present in any other type of organization? Answering that question might require some long and honest soul-searching, but your responses will help you gain an understanding of what is going on inside of one who has just joined the church. In a manner of speaking it will help you to "get inside the skin" of newcomers and have deeper empathy for the problems they face—the joys and disappointments that will be theirs. And this exercise in self-discovery will become even more effective if it becomes a group effort in which the findings are shared and pooled—and in which solutions are sought.

Let me share with you a listing of some of the reasons that a session of introspection brings to my mind. My being a Christian and belonging to one of God's visible churches provides and gives me (1) the opportunity to hear God's Word expressed, taught, shared, and explained, thereby strengthening my faith; (2) a place where I can receive the assurance of forgiveness, through both Word and Sacrament; (3) a sense of belonging to a caring family with common goals and interests; (4) an opportunity to worship and praise God with those who share that desire; (5) a place where I become an individual who is unique, rather than a number in a faceless society; (6) a solid, unchanging rock with a sense of continuity in a constantly and rapidly changing world; (7) a feeling of being wanted and needed, of having a purpose for living that makes life an adventure; (8) a sense of personal worth—not for what I possess but rather for what I am—coming both from God and from the community to which I belong; (9) a close fellowship with male and female alike, one that transcends the artificial barriers that exist in society; (10) a deep seated feeling of peace, joy, and fulfillment.

Those are some of the things that come to my mind, a list that is by no means exhaustive. Perhaps you have already thought of other reasons that could be added. But if we would look for similarities and group the reasons accordingly, we would find that the number could be reduced. We all possess some basic desires that are common to all mankind and that we must somehow meet if we are to achieve inner peace and joy.

That inner hunger has been described in general terms by a prophet who lived about 500 years before Christ. His name was Amos, and the words he wrote are in Amos 8:11-12: " 'Behold, the days are coming,' says the Lord God, 'when I will send a famine on the land; not a famine of bread, nor a thirst for water, but of hearing the words of the Lord. They shall wander from sea to sea, and from north to east; they shall run to and fro, to seek the Word of the Lord, but they shall not find it."

A nation of wanderers, searching for—we know not what! Certainly it is not a physical hunger or need that is the root cause of our restlessness, for we as a nation have an abundance of material possessions such as has been experienced by few—if any—of the civilizations that preceded ours. The quest for a better job, a more pleasing climate, or a high income may be the surface explanation for our mobility—but the real reason lies much deeper. It is the intangibles of life that prompt our search, for we have discovered that material possessions fail to still the yearnings generated from the inner depths of our being. An increased income, a new home, or a move to a different community does not bring us lasting happiness. Guilt still remains, even after many sessions on the psychiatrist's couch. Accumulated possessions have a way of disappearing overnight, and the drive for acquisition fails to still our hunger for recognition and purpose.

These are the needs that God has used to prepare the soil for the sowing of His Word—these are the yearnings that those who come to us want stilled and satisfied. And herein lie the clues to the kind of "nails" that can be used to secure them to the "birdhouse." They may be classified in five broad categories—I call them the five P's—Pardon, Peace, Power, Permanence, and Purpose. Now look at each one individually, both from the standpoint of problem and solution.

Guilt—how destructive that feeling can become. At times it is a burden so heavy that it practically immobilizes us. It can shatter relationships with others, and drive us into hiding— sometimes from ourselves. Even darkness fails to shield us from its devastating effects—tear-moistened pillows and twisted covers silently attest to that. Where can we find relief from this all-pervasive, common malady?

Society has tried to provide the requested solutions through several means. First, the assumption was made that guilt was the result of some unfair "Puritan ethic" that was based on a rigid set of standards known as the Ten Commandments. Therefore issue a declaration stating that the standards are no longer valid—give a stamp of approval to the concept of "doing your own thing" and presto—guilt feelings will vanish! Let the situation determine your actions or reactions, as you permit your personal definition of "love" to serve as your guide.

Millions subscribe to that philosophy—it touches all of us to some extent. Yet the relief that was promised has not materialized. Banning the written did not eradicate the unwritten inscribed within each of us—something called a conscience. The burden was still there.

Pychiatrists have tried to provide a solution through analysis. Probing and searching, they have tried to unearth someone in our past who could be blamed for our present misdeeds. Sometimes it was the parents who failed to properly carry out their function—we were overloved or underloved. In other cases it might be that one spouse was guilty of aggravating the other. Then there could always be the restrictive and oppressive nature of society and government that turned them into villains. Look long enough and the scapegoat could be found, no matter how dastardly the deed.

Who of us has not resorted to a similar form of reasoning in an effort to cleanse our inner being—and found it lacking. Excuses and passing the blame may provide momentary relief, but each of us must eventually admit to our own guilt as we honestly evaluate our motive and actions. No, even the professional humanistic counselor fails at this task.

True relief can only come to the Christian as we make the lonely pilgrimage to the foot of the cross and there hear our Savior declare on the behalf of you and me, "Father, forgive them; for they know not what they do" (Luke 23:34). The burden can be lifted for every child of God as we, who trust in His promises, hear our Father say to each of us; "I, I am He who blots out your transgressions for My own sake, and I will not remember your sins" (Is. 43:25). Our past vanishes, and the burden is destroyed by the same God whom David, experiencing the joy of forgiveness, described in these glowing terms: "He does not deal with us according to our sins, not requite us according to our iniquities. For as the heavens are high above the earth, so great is His steadfast love toward those who fear Him; as far as the east is from the west, so far does He remove our transgressions from us."

Yes, Christ has paid for every one of our wrongdoings, and God has declared us to be righteous in His sight. That is a promise—and an established fact—even though I may not feel forgiven at a particular moment. God's Word is trustworthy and never changes. On that I can depend.

What is true for me also holds for the newborn Christian. The problem is that he or she may not recognize that the search for pardon is over. That is why several important "nails" should be used at this time.

First, we should not assume that there is instant knowledge and acceptance of the destruction of the past. A number of years ago it was my privilege to be one of the instruments that the Holy Spirit used to bring about the rebirth of a 75-year-old gentleman who soon acquired the affectionate title of "Papa Don." He had been a bit of a rounder in his earlier years, and the twinkle was still very evident in his eyes. I accompanied him on his weekly jaunts to the pastor's class and witnessed his reaction to the explanation of God's law. Then he learned of Christ's love for him and of the forgiveness that was now his.

How hard that was for him to accept! I spent many hours explaining this to him again and again, always referring to the written promises of his Father. His common response was, "But Dick, I was a sinner for 75 years. I just don't see how He could forgive so much." It took a long time before that became reality to him. I often wonder if he would have wandered out the back door had I not been waiting at the front. Could this also hold true for many others who come to us? It takes more than a brief period of instruction—some patient handholding may also be called for. That is the shape of the first nail.

Second, there is the danger of confusing feelings with reality. The fact of my forgiveness depends on the inviolate nature of God's promise and not on my feelings. How I feel at any given moment is influenced by a number of factors: my mood, the weather, my physical health, job status, etc. Under the right circumstances guilt can still raise its ugly head. This is a very effective tool that is used by Satan to wreak havoc among God's people. How devastating this can be to the struggling spiritual infant! How easy it would be for Satan to cut the stragglers, those hanging on the fringes, from the rest of the flock!

The most effective "nail" is Christian fellowship, contact with others in a setting where bonds of trust are developed. There must be an openness that permits and encourages the sharing of feelings, doubts, fears, struggles—that helps the infant disciple to see that he is not alone or unique.

There must also be sharing of God's Word and the application of its precious promises to our everyday situations. The assurance of forgiveness and a destroyed past is a "nail" that must be "driven in" slowly, patiently, and with great care—but it is one that has great holding power.

But even the assurance of forgiveness and the beginning of a new life in Christ does not immediately solve all our problems and insure perfect inner peace. The old nature must be dealt with—the corrupt human flesh we all inherit from Adam and Eve. This flaw in our nature manifests itself as a natural tendency toward selfishness—we call it original sin. The result is an inner battle, a conflict between our high aspirations and that which we finally end up doing. St. Paul gives us a vivid description of that struggle in Rom. 7:18-19; "I can will what is right, but I cannot do it. For I do not do the good I want, but the evil I do not want is what I do."

We who are on the road to becoming mature disciples are aware of this war going on inside, understand it, and have learned to cope with and accept it. We have also found sources of strength that enable us to achieve an occasional victory. This may not be true for the newly won. Many have come from a life of self disappointment and now expect to leave all that behind and experience only inner peace and tranquillity. The shock of discovering a continuing struggle may lead them to feel that they are no longer Christian—may make them ashamed to be with others in the church—and could be the thrust that pushes them toward the back door.

Again, a strong bond of fellowship is a good part of the answer, a trusting relationship in which inner feelings can be revealed without fear of rejection or scorn. To do this requires an effort on our part, for it means that we will have to shed our "good Christian" mask. This is that serene outward countenance we display even when we are torn apart inside. It is the happy expression that a family puts on when they enter the church, even though they might have been quarreling ever since they arose that morning. It is the look that, when we see it on others, makes us question our Christianity—for we know what we are like inside, and we assume that the other person is different (even though we at that very moment may be projecting that same peaceful outward demeanor).

What feelings of failure must be present in these struggling spiritual infants as they observe the faces of those who occupy the surrounding pews on Sunday morning! I often wonder how many are "shaken loose" by this experience. This is a place for another "nail," that of understanding, sharing, and caring—the friendly and supporting arm around the shoulder. Somehow we must let them know that what is happening to them is normal—that it takes place in all of us.

But it is not enough to talk only about lost battles—there is also the necessity of explaining how victory can be achieved. They must learn how to face the reality of their inner weaknesses and hidden flaws while being led to the source of power that can help them change. In all probability this will be a new experience for them.

The members of today's society are reluctant to face reality. Instead, they want to escape. Alcohol becomes a universal panacea—drugs are taken in ever-increasing doses—hallucinogens are used to expand the subconscious—tranquilizers are found in most medicine chests—"downers" are taken to counteract "uppers" and vice versa. There is constant experimentation in the hope that a harmless agent will be found that will help us get away from ourselves and thereby find peace. Many have tried—and many have failed. Some of these failures have been used by God to prepare the soil. Some of these searchers end up on the doorstep of the church.

Within the church these searchers may discover that through God's power in the Gospel they are enabled to face reality and with His strength undergo change. Those of us who have been disciples for longer periods of time have experienced victories—we are familiar with the weapons that must be used—we know the necessary strategy. St. Paul shows us the way in Eph. 6:16-17: "[Take] the shield of faith, with which you can quench all the flaming darts of the evil one. And take the helmet of salvation, and the sword of the Spirit, which is the Word of God. Pray at all times in the Spirit, with all prayer and supplication."

The "nail" that is called for to strengthen these wobbly boards is the study of God's Word. All too often we view the course known as the pastor's class as being all-sufficient and regard confirmation as equivalent to graduation. The result is an attitude that views the Bible as a source of information and fails to recognize that it is at the same time a source of inspiration—an ongoing fountain of strength that we can turn to every day. To partake of this living water we must, in the words of a familiar prayer, "read, mark, learn, and inwardly digest" God's message to us as found in Holy Scripture. Here we find the nourishment that enables us to develop strong spiritual muscles—the nutrients that will give us an expanding skeletal frame. The problem is that we seldom turn to this source. Our "old Adam" helps us to procrastinate, to delay, to study everything but the Word.

More than admonition is needed if we are to motivate the procrastinating newcomer (or old-timer). What is needed is a web of mutual support—a necessity for most of us. Interesting Bible classes, good teachers, classes open to discussion and sharing, an invitation that says, "I will pick you up on Monday night"—these are the reinforcing nails that will bring to growing disciples a sense of peace while leading them to the source of power. This is the atmosphere in which growth can take place as the boards become ever more secure.

Secure boards, in an insecure world of unceasing change! It once required centuries for knowledge to double. Then doubling could be measured in generations or decades. Today it is a matter of a few years, and even that is constantly shrinking. What is new today is obsolete tomorrow. Everything is in a state of flux—customs, fashions, jobs, trends, and knowledge. How we long for just one thing that will remain stable, something to which we can cling as a sign of continuity! We hunger for a solid rock that will remain even after we are gone, something that will say, "I once walked on the face of this earth."

A sense of permanence—is there any way it can be achieved? We once thought that a name on the cornerstone of a building would do it. Today a network of well-placed charges of dynamite can reduce that monument to a pile of rubble in seconds. The marble gravestones may remain, but the memory of those whose names are inscribed soon fades. The search seems to lead only up blind alleys. But in that maze God sometimes finds the open heart, the fertile soil in which the seed will grow.

"Jesus Christ is the same yesterday and today and for ever" (Heb. 13:8). That is also our rock, one that will not be swept away, no matter how turbulent the stream of life may become. It is to Him that we turn as we try to shape our lives in a changing environment. It was a wise person who once said that life is like a bridge—it is something that you cross over, but it is not the place on which you build your house. If we could observe the brief span of our life from the viewpoint of eternity, we would see what a tiny blip it actually is on that endless line—and we would realize the futility of expending all of our energies on that portion, when so much lies ahead.

If only we could see things through God's eyes—realize that we are "aliens and exiles" (1 Peter 2:11). If only we could get a glimpse of the "Father's house" with "many rooms" described by Jesus in John 14:2. If only we could put things in proper perspective! Then change would become endurable, because we would have something that we could grasp.

Some of these "boards" come to us because they want to be nailed to something solid. They are tired of being adrift. They look to the church as a source of continuity, something that will remain relatively stable year after year. Does this then mean that we cannot change—at least in outward custom? Certainly adjustments can be made, but it must never be done for the sake of change alone. Make certain that circumstances justify—and members support—the innovation.

But there is one thing that must not change, namely the message that is proclaimed. The application may vary, but the content must always be the same. God's grace, His love, His instructions for living, His forgiveness—these stand forever in all truth and purity. Teach the Word from the pulpit, in the classroom, and through the home Bible class. Use every means at your disposal to place the feet of the trembling searchers on this solid rock. The Holy Spirit has provided us with the nail—it is up to us to use it. Drive it in firmly!

That leaves us with one need—the one that is perhaps most important of all. It is the one thing for which so many hunger and that is so important to us that its absence can destroy our sense of worth, our health, and even our lives. It is a purpose—or reason—for living. Possess a valid purpose, and life becomes an exciting adventure filled with happiness and fulfillment. Lose it, and you will find depression at your door. It happens to all of us—the mother whose children have all left home—the wage earner who has lost his job—the teenager who feels unwanted—the man or woman who has just retired—the elderly who find themselves in a nursing home. None of us are immune.

Where can I find a valid purpose for living? Society gives many answers. Accumulate material possessions that can then be passed on to your children, it has said, and then you will find fulfillment. That may satisfy for a while—until we observe the heartaches and quarreling that often result when inheritances are distributed. Make a name for yourself—build a reputation—and then people will look up to you. A solution for a moment—and then we retire, or are forgotten. Take care of your family—and then one day the nest is empty.

Dozens of solutions have been offered for that vexing problem—and all fail us when the need is the greatest. Suddenly the purpose on which we have built our entire existence vanishes, and we are left empty—feeling completely worthless. How often that stabbing pain strikes—and how often God uses personal calamity to crumble the rocks of resistance and thereby loosen the soil for the approaching sower. It is a hunger that lurks in many who come to us. There is a yearning for meaning that the world has not been able to fill. So they stand before us with hands outstretched, waiting for that hunger to be stilled. Many will wander off unless their need is met.

Only God can still that longing, and He has designated His church as the agency that will carry out the task. We have been assigned a mission—it is called the Great Commission. Go back to the previous chapter and read it again. Remember that we are told to make disciples—not only to bring them in but also to help them grow to maturity. Each one of us has a part in that task—each one of us has been equipped to carry out a portion of the assignment.

It is a purpose that transcends time and builds for eternity. It is the kind of task that lifts our eyes from the mundane and gives us a glimpse of the glory that lies ahead. It is a mission that is with us from the moment of birth until we draw our last breath. In carrying it out we begin to have what Jesus promised in John 10:10: "I came that they may have life, and have it abundantly." It is here that we finally achieve a lasting inner peace, fulfillment, and happiness. And it is this "nail" that will perhaps do more than any other to assure a lasting "hold." Use it we must. Just how is the subject of the next chapter.

Five separate "nails," each one able to strengthen the bond between the "board" and the "birdhouse." Use them all effectively, and the danger of having the "board" fall away is practically eliminated. Here they are, in summary form—five adhesives that should be provided:

(1) Someone assigned the responsibility for "hand-holding" during the crucial initial period.

(2) A Christian fellowship in which bonds of trust can be formed, sharing can take place, and inner feelings and struggles can be revealed.

(3) Friends from within the church who understand, share, and support.

(4) Opportunities for the study of God's Word in a number of different settings and themes, coupled with actively seeking attendance; emphasis on the bonding and strengthening that come through Baptism and Holy Communion.

(5) Assistance in finding purpose through discipleship.

God will provide the "hammer." It is up to us to use it, so that none might be lost. Are you driving home the nails with your gifts, the hammer, that God has provided for you? Look around you, I am sure that you know of loose boards that are in danger of falling off the house unless one or more nails are added. Others may be in need of initial fasteners. You have a task—now it is time to start pounding!

Chapter 10

Applying the Paint

At long last the birdhouse was completed. The final nail had been driven in, and now father and son stepped back to admire their handiwork. Some of the boards were slightly askew, and there was a gap here and there, but they still felt a touch of pride at what they had accomplished together. "Dad," the boy said, "I think that it needs some paint to cover up those stained boards, don't you?" "Yes," Dad replied, "that sounds like a good idea. Why don't you get some out of the basement."

The boy hurried off to the storeroom, where the paint was kept, and looked at all the cans there. None of the colors seemed appropriate, but he wanted to get it painted, so he chose a bright orange. His dad helped him remove the lid, and wanted to assist him in the task of stirring, for the pigments had settled to the bottom. But the boy was tired and becoming impatient, so he shrugged off his father's offer and instead applied the thin liquid that was on top. It ran down the side, leaving streaks and barely covering the surface.

The next day they put the birdhouse in a tree, but the color frightened off the intended guests, and the thin coating soon wore away, exposing the boards to the weather. In a short time the wood began to rot—and soon the birdhouse was no more.

How important "paint" is if the "birds" that abound in our neighborhoods are not only to be attracted to "God's birdhouse," but will also want to build there. What kind of "paint" will be required so that the "boards" will be protected from the ravages of a hostile environment? What "color" will be the most attractive—will offer the warmest visual invitation?

Such questions may appear to be trivial. "After all," you might say, "the 'birdhouse' has been built. Isn't that enough? If the 'birds' choose to ignore us, that is their problem." How easy it is to adopt that attitude, and how opposed it is to the concept of the Great Commission!

What kind of "paint" does God want us to use? What is the right "color," the one that will have the most "pulling power"? We find our answers in the description of the early church, particularly as recorded in Acts 2:42-47. Here are some of the most descriptive phrases from that section: "They devoted themselves to the apostles' teaching and fellowship, to the breaking of bread and the prayers." "All who believed were together and had all things in common." "Breaking bread in their homes, they partook of food with glad and generous hearts, praising God and having favor with all the people. And the Lord added to their number day by day those who were being saved."

Doesn't that sound exciting and attractive—like something that you would want to belong to? They were enjoying the favor of all people, not only because of their words, but also because of a life-style that gave credibility to their message. We can almost see the surrounding community watch this group that was so different from the norm of the day and hear them say: "Look how they care for one another!" As a result, they not only came to observe, but they also entered that "birdhouse" in droves.

It is still possible for that to happen today. In fact, we sometimes see it taking place. When it does, you can be sure that part of the secret of success is in using the right "paint." Let me illustrate by starting with a "color" called joy, the characteristic that—in the early church—is best described with the phrase, "glad and generous hearts."

A small boy was sitting beside his father in church one Sunday morning and, in a manner so typical of that age group, kept wiggling and squirming to the point of distracting those who were sitting nearby. Finally the father lost his patience and gave his son a whispered admonishment, followed by a not-so-gentle squeeze and shake. The physical pressure stopped the wiggling and squirming, but it was wounded pride that caused a tear to trickle down the little face.

The look of hurt and unhappiness was still clouding the boy's features as he approached the pastor after the service. "What is the matter, Bobby," asked the pastor, "why are you looking so glum?" "Well," replied the little parishioner, "it's pretty hard to be happy and holy at the same time."

It is hard to be happy and holy at the same time. How often we hear that sentiment being expressed, or see it being acted out in the lives of Christians with whom we rub shoulders in our community. Why should this be? Why the glum expression, when Christ has promised all His followers that, "I came that they may have life, and have it abundantly"

(John 10:10). What has happened to the joy that is ours to possess, the happiness that should be outwardly evident?

These are questions of major importance. How we look and act can have a profound effect on those who are outside the flock. They see us and observe our actions long before they hear our verbal expressions of faith. It is often their reaction to the former that will determine their response to the latter. A Chinese proverb states it quite simply: "What you are speaks so loudly that I cannot hear what you are saying." If we want to talk about the joy and happiness that is ours because we belong to Christ, then it should be plainly discernible to those around us.

This does not mean that we should have a constant ear-to-ear grin on our face. There are times when sorrow invades our existence and tears flow down our cheeks. We experience setbacks, and sometimes hardship becomes our lot. Emotions are still part of our being and on occasion send us on a roller-coaster ride that takes us through lows as well as highs. But no matter what the circumstances or the mood, we still know that beneath us are the everlasting arms of our Father. We are assured of His loving concern and presence. We are never alone. And in that promise we can find a sense of joy and inner happiness even in those moments when tears blur our vision.

To understand what we are trying to attain, it might be well first clearly to understand just what it is that we are looking for. What is happiness?

Happiness is a state of well-being and contentment. Someone has described it as a condition in which most of our thoughts are pleasant. It is not to be confused with pleasure, which is a gratification of the senses. It is possible to buy pleasure, fleeting though it may be, and for that reason it is more closely allied with material possessions. The same is not true of happiness. The quantity of your material possessions is not a measure of your inner well-being, nor will social status or a position of high prestige insure its presence. In fact, some of those who have the most and who receive the greatest adulation are also the most miserable.

Where can we find this elusive quality, the acquisition of which is the common goal of most of mankind? That is part of our search, isn't it? Its pursuit accounts for much of our aimless wandering and leads many to look at the one group that claims to have the answer—the Christian church. What they see can either arouse their curiosity and bring them into contact with the Gospel—or it can turn them away. That is why the "paint" is important.

Even the most casual observer must soon conclude that only a minority of those within the church seem to have a true sense of joy and peace. I am convinced that a majority would, if given the opportunity to be absolutely honest, say no when asked, "Are you happier as a Christian than you would be if you were not?" Several reasons might account for this attitude.

First, many are convinced that unhappiness is the lot of those who follow Christ. They hear our Lord tell us to take up our cross, and they immediately associate that with suffering that will rob them of joy. "The world will hate us," they are told—and visions of the "slings and arrows of misfortune" are brought to mind. Auditory problems plague them—one ear is partially deaf—and unfortunately they have the good ear turned toward the voice of the Law, while through the other there comes a garbled version of the Gospel. Therefore a serious mien becomes a fixed expression—the attitude of a *suffering* servant is their way of life.

Second, there are those who look upon their church membership as a form of fire insurance. Their church attendance and financial offerings become, in their eyes, premiums that must be paid—at least semiannually or annually—to forestall loss of protection. Payments are made reluctantly and at the last moment, and any increase in cost is met with loud protestations. Meanwhile, they look with envy at those who seem to be able to ignore possible future calamity, thinking of what could be saved in premium costs. Their only hope is that someday they will be able to collect the full face value of the policy, eternal life, for that would make all this "sacrifice" worthwhile. Meanwhile they suffer from day to day. For these, too, it is a way of life.

Third, some see God as a fence-builder who has erected a barrier around His people here on earth with the sole intent of preventing them from fully enjoying themselves. That chainlink boundary is held in place by 10 massive posts. Collectively these are called the Ten Commandments. The members of His church are clustered within, looking with envy at those who are outside the enclosure—who have freedom to do anything they want—who sip and savor every moment to its fullest—who live exciting lives and have a zest for living. "If only I could be out there," they say, as they peer with great longing through the intervening links. Occasionally they attempt to scale the barricade, and it is only the fear of punishment that brings them back. In the meantime their downcast facial expression gives ample evidence of the feelings that are inside.

Fourth, there are some who are lurking on the fringes, but who repel all attempts to bring them inside the circle of fellowship. Some are there because of family pressures or pride. They are following a custom that extends back through branch after branch of their family tree—they belong to the You Name It church, just like mom and dad and grandpa and grandma and others. The requirement for continuity is met just as long as the name exists on the membership rolls. Out there with them are the loners and those who feel awkward and out of place. All of these peer inside but are afraid to make the commitment that will take them to the center. They have never actually tasted God's goodness in full measure, and so happiness eludes them.

Fifth are those who exert the strongest and most persistent tug on my heart—those who tried and failed and now feel that they have nothing to contribute and consequently are worthless. Theirs is a true sadness—one that should receive the highest priority as we seek solutions. Theirs are willing hands that may have either been inadvertently or intentionally rebuffed. Now their fingers lie idle in their lap, while their heart grieves silently at the thought of being unable to serve the Lord who is loved. Of all those mentioned, the reaction of this group is most easily justified.

There they are—some of the reasons, as I perceive them, for the shabby exterior appearance of our "birdhouse" when viewed by the hovering flock of "birds" that is searching for a resting place. You may have even more in mind. But it does no good to analyze—and then complain about peeling paint and stained boards—unless we at the same time search for ways to repair the damage and apply a protective coating of the proper paint. I would like to go back and do that for each of the five categories, examining them individually.

First, let's go back to those who feel that straight, firm lips, with a slight downturn at the corners, are standard Christian equipment. For some that idea may have its roots in early childhood—and in the feeling that was vocalized by little Bobby in the incident related earlier in the chapter. Bits of that, "Be quiet! You are disturbing the worship of others!" are bound to remain hidden in the recesses of the mind and affect future attitudes. For others it might be a false sense of piety that calls into question any sign of humor or outward gaiety on the church premises. They find it hard to distinguish between frivolity and true joy.

But that sad exterior probably results most from a misconception in regard to something that is thought of as "cross bearing." In their minds there is a direct relationship between that concept and a glum expression. To them it is pure and simple cause and effect. They make their error in assuming that having the burden must result in unhappiness. While it is true that Jesus did tell us to take up our cross, He did not say, "Take up your cross and follow Me—because I want to make sure that you will be unhappy." What we do find Him saying is that "there is more happiness in giving than in receiving" (Acts 20:35 TEV). That cross, which could represent either giving or giving up, can—when shouldered—bring to us quite the opposite of what we might expect. In the lifting of that burden we may find that for which we yearn—the elusive quality called happiness. I know, for it happened to me.

The first 29 years of my life were spent in searching, though in varying degrees of intensity. I had been gathered up and nailed as a "board" to that "birdhouse" when a mere babe in arms, and though the nails had held, there were moments when this board shook and rattled under the buffeting of storms. Had you peeked into the church you would have found me on the fringes, reluctant to make a commitment to taking that first inward step, yet curious enough to keep looking. Then I met Pastor F. Waldo Boettcher, who did two things. First he spent time with me, hours in which we explored the depths of God's Word. But he did not stop there. He next "took me by the hand and led me inside"—by asking me to teach a Sunday school class and sing in the choir.

Reluctant? Of course! Hesitant? My dragging feet ploughed twin furrows! Frightened? My kneecaps rattled! But he never let go of my hand as he continued to express confidence in my ability. There finally came the Sunday when the first timid step of service was taken. Through that act—and in those moments—I sipped the nectar of a joy that had eluded me all my life. On that day my life was changed, and it has never reverted back to what it once had been. How often I have thanked God for that servant of His who took the time and had the patience to put my foot on the first rung of a ladder. What resulted has been a climb that has always been directed upward, and has led me into ever higher realms of happiness through service.

"Paint" tinted with the essence of a hue called joy—how we need that if our "birdhouse" is to be attractive. To apply it to "boards" that bear the stains of misconceptions and erroneous assumptions requires the broad and steady brushstrokes of patient and persuasive teaching. Attitudes, deeply ingrained from a lifetime of practice, are hard to change. It can happen if they are brought into firm contact with the Gospel again—and again—and again. God should be reintroduced to them as that which He really is—our kind and loving Father, who wants us to be happy. True, burdens may come our way, but only because He permits it, so that we might be led closer to Him and to our earthly goal of peace and joy.

The holders of the "fire insurance policies" present a different kind of problem. Theirs is not so much a matter of attitude as it is of feeling—the impression that there are no temporal benefits to being a Christian. In fact, they view church membership as something that only costs them in one way or another—and never pays any earthly dividends. With that mindset, the envy they feel when they view the carefree lifestyle of their neighbors is easy to understand.

Again it becomes a matter of education, but this time in the true meaning of redemption and salvation. That may even take some rethinking on our part, perhaps a different approach to the way the topic of Christ's saving work is presented. It was John who gave us a description of that work when he wrote in 1 John 4:14: "We have seen and testify that the Father has sent His Son as the Savior of the world." Jesus was sent not only to save us from our sins but also to save us from ourselves.

Luther describes that work so well in his explanation of the Second Article in the Small Catechism. It might be good to quote a major portion of that beautiful statement as a way of refreshing our memories:

"I believe that Jesus Christ, true God, begotten of the Father from eternity, and also true man, born of the virgin Mary, is my Lord, who has redeemed me, a lost and condemned creature, delivered me and freed me from all sins, from death, *and from the power of the devil*, not with silver and gold but with His holy and precious blood and with His innocent sufferings and death, in order that *I may be His*, live under Him in His kingdom, *and serve Him in everlasting righteousness, innocence, and blessedness*" *(The Book of Concord,* Tappert Edition, Small Catechism, Creed 4).

What is encapsulated in the words *redeemed* and *salvation*? It is inadequate to think of them as meaning *only* deliverance from the punishment of hell. We need to be saved also from ourselves—we need to be saved from habits that can bind us just as surely and completely as the strongest of chains—we long to be rescued from temptations that surround us—we tremble under the stinging lash of our fears and anxieties and await deliverance—we want to be freed from follies, mistakes, impulses, and errors in judgment. In each one of these cases Jesus offers us salvation. Only He could offer and fulfill the invitation to, "Come to Me, all who labor and are heavy laden, and I will give you rest" (Matt. 11:28). Only He could promise: "Lo, I am with you always, to the close of the age" (Matt. 28:20b).

He is with me every second, day and night—and with His presence is also His power. I am different because I am a Christian, not because of some Herculean effort on my part, but because Christ has given me the power to change. In so many ways He has saved me from myself. The result has been a life that is freed from some of the enslaving bonds of my corrupted human flesh. He helps me to stifle my natural selfish impulses, to overcome a tendency to procrastinate, to face the future with confidence. Because of that my life is better here and now—and in addition there is the "frosting on the cake," an eternity in the presence of God.

In view of all this, there is aroused in me a deep-seated feeling of gratitude and love for God, who has so selflessly given of Himself for me. I want to do something for Him, not because He demands it but chiefly because He has placed within me the deep desire and the strength to serve Him (Phil. 2:13). Deeds performed and material gifts presented no longer present the image of an "insurance premium" that is paid under protest. Instead, they become an offering of love given under an inner compulsion.

Covering these "boards" with that "paint" displaying the color chip "joy" again calls for patience, understanding, and an effort to teach the full meaning of salvation. Time must be spent on the subject of the sanctified life so that people will understand the power that the Holy Spirit can bring to bear as we wrestle with the one called "me." One of the best places this can take place is in a Bible class, where there is contact not only with the Word but also with fellow Christians involved in similar struggles.

The "fenced in" group presents still another problem in bringing about an understanding of what God's true intentions are. To accomplish that requires that we wrestle with a "why" question, namely "Why did God give us the Law?" Our immediate reaction is to answer, "As a form of deprivation—or to punish us. It is part of the price that we must pay for being Christians."

Is that observation and conclusion correct? Does it match the description of God that we find in the Bible? A diligent search reveals that the answer to both questions must be no. John says that God is love—a form of love that in Greek is called *agape*—which means that He has a continual selfless concern for our welfare. In addition, Jesus has promised life in the fullest measure. The picture of the Law as a restrictive and joy-destroying set of rules does not fit that description of God and His intentions for us. Why, then, did He erect that "fence"?

I have spent thousands of hours in the cockpits of aircraft, and many of those have been devoted to careful observation of the dozens of gauges on the instrument panel. Careful attention to that task was required, because the first indication of a malfunction was usually to be found there. At first there was hopeless confusion, primarily because of the wide variety of instruments and readings. But the manufacturer did much to simplify the readings by marking each dial with a red line. All that was then required was a quick glance to determine the position of the needle in relation to that very evident mark. If it remained on the proper side you could relax—while an indicator either approaching or crossing that line called for an immediate heart-thumping response.

The position of that line was established by the manufacturer, for he was very familiar with the operating limits of that component. He had been responsible for the initial design and therefore marked the limits of stress so as to prevent destruction.

The Ten Commandments serve the same function for each one of us. God designed us, and He knows what can wreak havoc and destruction in our lives. It was out of a concern for our welfare and happiness that there came that set of 10 "red lines." God established safe operating limits for you and me and then gave us some clearly defined boundaries of operation. "Go beyond this," He says, "and you will hurt yourself, perhaps even running the risk of self-destruction." The Law gives me freedom, for it tells me what I can do and, what is equally important, when I should stop.

The fence (or curb) is still there, but it serves an entirely different purpose from that which the devil leads us to believe is true. Imagine that you have just been placed somewhere on a smooth, level field—on an inky black night so dark that you cannot see your hand when it is six inches in front of your face. In the center of that field is an abandoned missile silo with sheer sides extending 300 feet downward. You know of this pit and are aware that there is nothing to warn you of its presence. At this point you are turned loose and are told that you have absolute freedom to do anything you want. Would you feel free? Absolutely not! In all probability you would be paralyzed by fear, grasped by a terror shouting in your mind's ear that the next step would take you over the brink and plunge you to your death.

How different it would be if a 10-foot sturdy chain link fence were erected around that underground silo! Now suppose you were out there in those same conditions, and were again given freedom to follow your desires. Freedom of movement is now possible, for you would know that the fence was there to prevent an accidental death plunge.

Just so it is with the Law. The Christian is not imprisoned on the inside—we are the ones who are freely roaming the plains of life. True, there is a fence, but it surrounds the pit of destruction. Within that enclosure are those who are trapped—enslaved to drugs or alcohol, captives of their material possessions, imprisoned behind the bars of sexual lust and excesses. Their moans and cries of distress can be heard as we approach the brink. Those who are on the outside, the followers of Christ, are the ones who are free—for God has let them see the boundary fence, He has told them when to stop.

Applying the "joy paint" requires many strokes of the Gospel brush, drawing again and again the picture of God, who is only concerned for our temporal and eternal welfare. As this takes place, it should slowly become apparent that the Law is an instrument of God's love (protecting us and letting us know what is pleasing to Him), not an outpouring of His wrath. With this will come a change in attitude as envy is replaced by gratitude.

What about those who have erected a fence of their own making that keeps them from joining the circle of fellowship within "God's birdhouse"? If there is one characteristic common to all of those mentioned in the fourth category it is *fear of commitment*. They are afraid to "sign on the dotted line"—to volunteer and take one step forward from the ranks—because they feel uncertain about the outcome.

Part of this hesitancy is a result of the philosophy that became part of our troubled society during the past several decades. The experience of the Vietnam war caused many to look askance on any request to offer oneself for service. The uncertainty of tomorrow because of a nuclear threat made a "live for today and take care of myself first" attitude seem very natural. But much of it, especially on the part of the Christian, is due to a basic mistrust of God. We are afraid to trust Him with our future. Let me explain.

Power can be useful, but it also can be frightening. Do you remember the first time you sat behind the wheel of a car and were asked to move it forward? Remember the timid application of pressure to the accelerator pedal? I well recall a similar incident in my life—my checkout in jet aircraft.

I was no novice to flying when all of this transpired some 26 years ago—but the 3,000 hours of flying time had been acquired in various propeller-driven aircraft. My initial reaction to a small fighter-trainer was one of excitement coupled with tinges of apprehension. All too soon the seven hours of dual time passed, and the day came when the instructor climbed out—and I was on my own! Fright gripped me when I reached the end of the runway. I found myself going through the pre-takeoff checklist once—and twice—and was ready for the third try when the tower informed me that there was someone behind me and that, unless there was trouble, I better get going. Why was I so reluctant to take the next step and advance the throttle to 100% power? Because of fear that I would lose control. Speed builds up slowly in a prop aircraft—things happened much faster in a jet. And so I questioned my ability to stay on top of everything—to do all that was required in those first seconds of flight.

That is the feeling we get when we encounter the spiritual power that God offers to us, isn't it? There are times when we feel moved by all that our Lord has done for us, and we respond by offering our lives in His service. We bravely say, "Here I am Lord; I commit myself to You. Take me and use me in any way that You want—but..." But don't make me move—don't make me leave my occupation—don't this—don't that. We are willing to trust God with anything—except our future. Somehow we get the feeling that He will place us in positions that will cause us unhappiness—that will make our lives miserable. I still feel that way at times, in spite of being able to look back on a lifetime in which that never happened.

So often I am reminded of the trust that is accorded fellow human beings, but is denied God. I have made hundreds of instrument approaches in aircraft, many under conditions when the cloud ceiling was so low that the ground became visible mere seconds before touchdown. Often these approaches were made under the guidance of Ground Controlled Approach, following the voice commands of controllers on the ground who were monitoring the flight path on radar screens. Changes in altitude and heading were given verbally as this unknown individual tried to keep our aircraft on the unseen line that led to the end of the runway. Follow instructions with precision, and the lights outlining the landing strip would be directly ahead of us when we broke out of the overcast.

I would never have thought of questioning the verbal commands that I was receiving—even though I had no way of determining the abilities of the one directing me. Experience had taught me to trust, and I had faith in the training and the equipment.

How different it becomes when I deal with God! The fog obscuring our vision as we "fly" through life is impenetrable. We have no way of knowing what the next minute has in store for us, let alone the next day—or the next month—or the next year. The only one who can see down that path is our Father, and it is His desire that we have a perfect landing. In addition, He wants to steer us around all the storms that lie in our path, so that our flight will be smooth. Isn't it strange that we are so reluctant to trust Him—when we commit our lives into the hands of unknown pilots and radar operators every time we board a commercial aircraft? Could it be that Satan is more powerful than we think?

For those lurking on the fringes, the paint must be applied by hand. We who have tasted and found fulfillment must be willing to stretch out our hand and gently lead the hesitant into the fold. It is up to us to demonstrate—with our own lives and testimony—that God's promise to lead us will take us to the promised "green pastures and still waters." That is no small task, for it requires faith and courage—trust and conviction—to dispense with the "buts" in our lives. But as we all start to walk hand in hand down the Spirit-directed paths that lie ahead, the invitation given through David in Ps. 34:8, "Taste and see that the Lord is good!" will become a reality and will lead to ever-increasing joy and peace.

Now for the final group—those who tried and failed, or whose efforts may have been rebuffed or rejected. These are the ones who deserve our heartiest support and most tender understanding. Some of them we already know. In our minds we have classified them as too old—too young—completely lacking in ability—from the wrong kind of background—wearing the wrong kind of clothes— hair too long, or too short—etc. They belong to a category that we label "just not able to do anything around the church." They never make the nominations list—and are never asked to serve in any capacity.

There may have been a time when they tried, but their feeble attempts to gain attention were quickly brushed aside. The resulting hurt pushed them into the shell where they now sit, afraid to venture out into a church that has the power to again inflict the pain of rejection.

Sometimes these individuals come to our attention as we note their apparent lack of enthusiasm and happiness. Our natural response to this condition is to say something like, "What is bothering you? You should be happy! Look at all that God has done for you." It is true that our Lord has done much for them, as He has for each one of us. It is also true that the knowledge of His loving care and providence should fill our hearts with joy. But there is more to it than that! We will never experience true joy, peace, and happiness unless we can give in response to God's goodness. That is what Jesus meant when He said, "It is more blessed to give than to receive" (Acts 20:35).

This was brought home to me very vividly several months ago. Travels through the western states made it possible for us to visit Rajneeshpuram, the ranch that is the headquarters for Indian guru Bhagwan Shree Rajneesh. I was—and am—totally opposed to the philosophy of life that he expounds, but what we saw fascinated me. Several thousand young men and women live in this community where they are combining their efforts to carve a veritable oasis out of semi-desert grazing land. They come from the middle and upper strata of society and the most are well educated. Yet they come here, ask to become a disciple of Bhagwan, and promise, if accepted, to make a financial "offering" and work 12 hours per day, 7 days a week, for months on end. The work they do is demanding and often backbreaking as they transform the harsh landscape, build their quarters, and tend the fields and livestock. They are free to leave anytime they desire—yet they remain, and the hundreds of faces I observed all reflected the same sense of happiness and peace. When asked about vacations the common reply was, "Our work is our recreation."

I left there filled with both a curiosity as to why they felt this way—and a desire to somehow infect the members of "God's birdhouse" with the same "virus." What hold does Bhagwan have over his followers? I believe that it is nothing more than letting them experience the joy of giving. How necessary it is that the disciples of Christ have that same experience! To deprive them of that opportunity is to deprive them of fulfillment.

To reach that goal requires a two-pronged attack. First, there is the task of helping all identify the unique spiritual gift with which God has blessed them. Together with this is the second assignment, that of finding work for each to do. This requires creative thinking on the part of the entire congregation, with perhaps a new philosophy on how to get things done. Some congregations have already embarked on this endeavor. The success that these pioneers are experiencing is ample demonstration of the effectiveness of this particular paint in attracting the neighborhood flocks.

A word of caution in regard to the way in which this giving takes place: There is a tendency to think of financial giving as the way in which we make our offering to God. There is an element of truth in that statement if we but replace "*the* way" with "one of the ways." The problem with gifts that are placed in the offering plate is that the giver is too far removed from the receiver. Often the money flows into the treasury and is then dispensed for various projects, some of which we may oppose. As a result, we are left with anger and/or disappointment rather than with a good feeling inside.

The growing disciple needs something called "positive feedback." If that is to happen, then the presenter must be in the position where the effects of the donated labor can be observed. This means that a spoken thank-you should be heard, a pat on the back must be felt. In the ideal world this would not be necessary, but we have not as yet arrived at that state. To summarize, we need something besides the offering plate if we are to satisfy our charitable impulses. At the same time we must recognize the need for positive feedback that still exists in most Christians.

There can be little doubt that the color of the "paint" is important. But there is another function that this coating must perform, namely that of protecting the "boards" from the onslaught of the elements. Again we get the clue from the description of the early church quoted earlier. There we are pointed to the prime ingredients: "They devoted themselves to the apostles' teaching and fellowship, to the breaking of bread and the prayers."

Right back to where we have been so often of late—the study of the apostles' teaching in the Bible—the need for the strong bonds of fellowship—the breaking of bread in the Sacrament of the Altar—prayer. Four ingredients that, if present, will protect the "boards" that make up our "birdhouse" from the most vicious assaults that Satan can mount.

What does this amount to in a practical sense? Our paint will be both attractive and protective if we:

1. Have good strong Bible classes that place a heavy emphasis on the Gospel.

2. Develop bonds of caring and sharing fellowship, in which there is the trust and freedom to reveal inner struggles—and the confidence to

share victories that have been achieved.

3. Help everyone who is part of the "birdhouse" search for—and find—their own special spiritual gift.

4. Create a network of avenues of service, so that everyone has an opportunity to participate and will have available the means to personally render a service both to God and the neighbor.

5. Recognize the true source of fulfillment and teach others about the need to give.

6. Do lots of patient hand holding, encouraging, praising, and confessing—reaching back to those on the remotest of the fringes.

7. Ask God to provide the motivation, the power, and the blessing on all you do.

Chapter 11

Erecting the Birdhouse

The birdhouse was finally completed! The boards were nailed together, the paint was brushed on, and now father and son stepped back to view their project and breathed a sigh of relief. The result of their combined efforts was carefully carried to a corner of the garage where the paint could dry undisturbed.

The next evening the father reminded the son of the task that still remained—a pole must be found that could be used to properly display their handiwork. But other activities beckoned, and the boy flung a hasty, "We'll do that tomorrow, Dad," as he ran to join the gang. As so often happens, that promised tomorrow never arrived, and today the birdhouse still sits in the corner, while overhead flocks of birds fly past, searching for a home.

It is not enough to just build a birdhouse—it must also be set up. A support item is necessary because it elevates the product of our labors into the realm of the birds—up where they live, and move, and have their being—up where they can see and use this carefully prepared resting place. And just as this is true for our humanly constructed "masterpiece," so it also holds for the spiritual haven that is fashioned through the cooperative efforts of God, you, and me. The question is, "What does the 'pole' look like?"

Somehow we must make "God's birdhouse" visible to those whom we are trying to attract. We have to elevate it into the world in which they live. To do that takes more than impressive structures, manicured lawns, large parking lots, and commercial advertisements. These may play a part but, because of their impersonal nature, will always be relegated to a minor role when results are evaluated. To be effective we must reach out with a personal touch. It is not enough to hear the surrounding community say, "Look how they love one another." We should at the same time be involved in their lives to the extent that they will also feel compelled to exclaim, "Look how they love us!"

The name of that needed "pole" is *outreach*. The first place where we are apt to go to find that needed construction item is in the "storage area" displaying the sign EVANGELISM above the gate. "That is the task of the evangelism committee," we are apt to say, as we run off to join the gang that is passing by. As a result, the search for the pole is usually forgotten, and the "birdhouse" continues to sit unnoticed in the corner. When and if our Father reminds us of that which must still be accomplished we can always respond with a, "It is in the hands of a committee. Please don't bother me."

Outreach—making our church visible and inviting to those in the surrounding community—requires much more than evangelism, even when Gospel-sharing teams are faithfully meeting and going out every week. The hand that reaches out has many fingers—in fact, there is one for each member of that church. Furthermore, these come in many shapes and sizes, even more than the normal five that we have on each hand. God has carefully designed, shaped, and has a use for, every single one of these. An effective outreach results when each is used in accordance with the planned intent of the Designer.

Evangelism teams are important, but do you remember the illustration of the obstetrician of an earlier chapter? We only need a relatively small number of those skilled in assisting in the delivery of the reborn infants. Seed must be sown, but the ground must first be cultivated if efficient use is to be made of the efforts of the sower. Furthermore, the growing plants need continual care if the fruit is to grow and be harvested.

Soil preparation is of extreme importance, as anyone who has ever planted a garden, seeded a lawn, or tilled the ground can readily testify. Maybe that explains why it is that relatives or friends are responsible for most of the souls brought to Christ every year. It is their persistent witness to their faith in Jesus as Savior that ultimately penetrates and cracks the most difficult of soils. In many cases this has meant years of patient waiting, standing by until God had everything in readiness. Of all the fingers, this is the one that is perhaps the longest and strongest of the lot. And yet, they are all only one link in God's chain, as you shall see.

Sometimes it is helpful to think about the means that God uses to bring the human being into His fold. There is a natural tendency to picture the whip of the Law being used to drive individuals into the waiting arms of the Savior—a milling herd being driven and cajoled toward the gate that leads to heaven.

This may be true to nature, but it is not the method used by our Maker. He operates in a different way.

The method He uses is described in two places in the Gospel of John. In John 6:44 Jesus tells the Jews: "No one can come to Me unless the Father who sent Me *draws* him." In John 12:32 He says: "I, when I am lifted up from the earth, will *draw* all men to Myself." He draws them—that is the method He uses! In so doing He often uses the gifts He has given to His people. I like to think of it in terms of "God's Living Links of Love"—a chain formed from the seven spiritual gifts listed in Chapter 8 of this book. Let me illustrate.

One of the projects in my grade-school days was making paper chains. Narrow strips of paper, all of equal length, were first cut from construction paper that came in various colors. The ends of each strip were then glued together to form a circle. If each strip was interlinked with another before fastening, the result was a chain of paper links. Sometimes these chains became quite long.

Now let your imagination try to picture God's chain. Picture for yourself a young couple with the unlikely names of Elmer and Martha, proud parents of two young children. Theirs is a close-knit family, but one that has had little time for God. Invitations have come their way over the years, but all have been rejected with a friendly—but firm—no.

This family now moves into your community. It is a rainy day, and the high humidity makes even light activity uncomfortable. Living across the street is a member of the local church. This woman has been blessed by God with the gift of giving. She observes the struggle, and obeys her natural impulse to go over and help. The early afternoon is spent in helping the newcomers get scattered belongings into the proper rooms. Finally she offers to go home and prepare dinner for an exhausted foursome—an invitation that is gladly accepted.

It is a very grateful couple who push themselves away from the table that evening. They are also filled with curiosity, and naturally ask why their newfound friend would want to do all of this. "Well," she replies, "I just like to do things for others. God has done so much for me that I want to repay His generosity in this way." Just one short reference that connects a kind act with God—that is all. No sermon—no presentation of the Gospel—no church. But God uses this link labeled "giving" to initiate the formation of His living chain of love.

Months go by—and things are not going as well as Elmer and Martha had hoped. The children are having trouble adjusting to school—the weather has been gloomy for days on end—the job does not meet expectation—and depression sets in. Another member from the church lives in the next block—one who has the gift of encouraging. He has gotten to know these newcomers and notices their downcast expression. He senses that things are amiss, and so he visits them one evening. The hours seem to fly by as this gifted individual slowly disperses the cloud of gloom that had enveloped them. Gradually his words of hope and comfort restore their good spirits, and he helps them to again catch the vision of the light at the end of the tunnel. Beaming faces express gratitude more effectively than words as he leaves. He shakes their hands and then says, "There are times when I also struggle with my emotional lows, but I always know that I am in God's hands, and that He cares for me." One simple sentence—but with that a link called "encouragement" is added to the chain.

A short while later Martha unexpectedly becomes ill and finds herself in the local hospital. In the church is a woman who was granted the gift of showing mercy. She expresses the inner desire that this generates by visiting the sick every week. She scans the list of those newly admitted as she enters the hospital that afternoon, and notices that Martha's name is followed by "no church affiliation." She stops at her bedside, starts a conversation, and before long her empathy and expressed sympathy are having a positive effect on Martha. As she gets ready to leave she asks if there would be any objection to a brief prayer. There being none, she bows her head and says, "Thank You, Lord, for leading me to Martha today—and please, Father, keep her in Your care so that she will soon be home again. In Jesus' name. Amen." Nothing long or profound, but very effective as the third link in the expanding chain—this one titled "showing mercy."

But before leaving, this woman pauses and says, "Martha, I noticed that you have no church home. As you now know, I belong to a church, and it is like another family to me. Would you mind if someone came over to your home some evening and described our church and what we believe?" For the third time Martha was hearing God's name mentioned in connection with an act of kindness, and her curiosity was aroused. She gave her wholehearted consent to the visit.

The woman returned to the church and reported on her visit to the secretary. Now within this church there was also a woman who had the gift of leadership. Using this attribute to the fullest, she had organized a group of individuals who were interested and motivated as evangelists. She scheduled all their weekly calls and, noting the openness of Martha and Elmer to a visit, asked two of her most gifted presenters to make the visit to their home on an agreed-upon evening. Though way in the background, this act of service was used by God to form the fourth link. Attached to it was the name "leadership."

The team had no trouble gaining entry into the home that night. In fact, Martha and Elmer were sitting there, awaiting their arrival. Bonds of friendship were quickly formed, and before long the seed was being sown on soil that had undergone months of tilling. For the first time there fell upon those waiting ears the message of a Father's love and of His Son's sacrifice—all on their behalf and for their benefit. But it was a story that was new to them, and so they asked for time to think about what they had heard. The fifth link had now been forged, branded with "teaching" and solidly attached to the other four. And now the drawing and tugging could be detected by this young couple. Slowly the living chain, initially attached through that first link so many months before, was pulling them into the arms of a waiting Father.

Before they left, arrangements were made to pick up Elmer, Martha, and the two children at 9:00 a.m. on the following Sunday and take them to church. That moment quickly arrived, and soon the family found itself at the church entrance. There they were met by an usher, one who had been richly endowed with the gift of serving. He immediately took the new arrivals in hand and, using his endowed instincts to the utmost, soon had them feeling very much wanted and at home. They were introduced to others, taken to the guest register, shown the hymnal, had the bulletin and order of service explained, and led to a pew where they would feel comfortable. By the time the service started they had the impression that they were royalty, the most important people on earth. Unknown to them, God had added the sixth link to His chain, one that to the human may look ordinary and unimportant, but to Him so vital. It bore the label "serving."

That morning the pastor, who was a gifted expository preacher with the ability to make God's Word come alive—he had the gift of prophecy—presented an inspiring message. That morning, as Martha and Elmer sat in the pew, the Holy Spirit used that Gospel message to open their hearts, and Christ entered in. That morning "prophecy," the seventh link, was added—God's chain composed of living links of love was completed—and He pulled Elmer, Martha, and the two children into His bosom.

God's living links of love, seven loops that He throws out into our communities much as a lifeguard tosses an inflated innertube out to a struggling swimmer—seven links that He uses to suspend our "birdhouse" so that it is elevated to the height at which the "birds" are flying—living links—human links—you and I—that is the kind of material He uses to form the chain that is so effective in drawing others to Christ. It is through this means that His "birdhouse" is built.

Every link is important. Cut any one of the seven and the chain is broken. All are vital to the successful completion of God's rescue mission. One of those links is you, just as I am another. Never picture yourself as being unimportant or worthless. Your presence and your efforts are very necessary in the Master's plan. But it is also necessary that you discover which of those links is you. Misconceptions can lead to guilt and unhappiness, as I well know.

As mentioned earlier, the initial encounter that I had with the joy of giving had a profound effect on my life. It left me with a deep desire to devote my life and my efforts to my Lord. At first it appeared that this could only be accomplished if I entered the pastoral ministry. However, the doors that God opened before me always seemed to lead to engineering, so that became the course I followed. Apparently thwarted in one direction, I turned to others. Sunday school, Bible classes, stewardship, offices within the congregation—I became involved in everything.

But one task was avoided, and that was evangelism. An introvert by nature, shy in the company of another person, afraid of "small talk," the very thought of going out to a strange home frightened me. Yet the need was always present, and my avoidance brought with it feelings of guilt. No matter if I was busy every night of the week in many church-related activities—"it" was still there, a specter that haunted me. As the years went by I finally forced myself to participate in organizations in which making calls was required. The day even came when not only going out but also training others became a full-time assigned task.

Now I was going out not just once, but 10 or more times per week. You would think that the guilty feelings would have vanished. Such was not to be—one set disappeared, only to be replaced by another. Now I was bothered by my reluctance to carry out that mission. "Why," I would ask myself, "do I pray that nobody will be home? Why do I feel relieved when no one comes to the door—when my trainees are often expressing genuine disappointment? Why do I want the snow to pile up so that the visits will have to be canceled? What is wrong with me—is my faith so weak that I cannot do what God asks of me?" How those questions plagued my conscience and disturbed my inner peace. The burden of guilt became overpowering.

It was while in the midst of this struggle that the nature of God's mission finally became clear to me. Making disciples involved more than just baptizing—we were also directed to teach. He not only wants them to be brought in—He also wants the infants nurtured and fed so that they will grow to maturity. Accomplishing that requires the full utilization of all of the seven gifts with which God has endowed His people.

I sometimes think of it in terms of the seven different molds, or "cookie cutters," that our Lord uses to shape His people. In looking back I can now see what happened. For much of my life I—and others—had tried to force me into a mold shaped like evangelism, and it failed to fit. Of course it pinched—and squeezed—and hurt—and the more pressure was applied, the worse it became. I was formed differently. My mold is teaching—it fits, and it is where I am most comfortable.

I shall never forget the night when all of this became apparent to me. It happened while I was on a small stage, explaining the cookie-cutter concept to members of a congregation. As I stamped a fictitious character into the wrong mold that evening I looked down—and suddenly saw myself. In that instant I understood—and 25 years of guilt slid from my shoulders. For the first time I felt clean inside and at peace with myself. Was it any wonder that hymns of praise and thanksgiving rang through my mind for hours on end?

Now I understand my feelings of reluctance—it was God's way of telling me that He could use me more effectively in other kinds of service. Now I understand my desire for anything related to teaching—the feeling of joy that accompanies the accomplishment of that task—the results that often follow. That is where God wants me to direct my efforts—He has given me that gift and wants that link put into the chain at the point where it will do the most good. This does not mean I cannot be used as an evangelist—or for any other task—but it does mean that it will never be as comfortable or as inviting as teaching. The difference is that I now no longer am plagued by guilt because I do not have an equal desire for all forms of service.

The same is true of all the other gifts that are mentioned. Some people just naturally give you "the shirt off their back," and it seems so easy for them. The same is not true for me, and I know why. Giving is not my gift. It is not as though I hoard my material possessions—but there is always a slight struggle before I part with them. Hospital visits also bother me—showing mercy is not second nature for me. I do it, but it requires a high resolve. For others this is an effortless task.

Now do you see why discovering your gift is so necessary?

That knowledge will help you to understand yourself—it will help you direct your efforts—and it just might make some of that guilt disappear, a needless burden that could be weighing you down.

It also explains why building "God's birdhouse" is a cooperative venture in which all the boards are necessary and are used. In looking at those boards, do not forget that the pastor is one of them. He has also been singularly gifted by our Creator and is plagued with the same kinds of desires and apprehensions that bother all of us. That may help you to understand why some tasks are hard for him to carry out and others are done well with very little effort. It also points out why it is necessary that we all work together to complete the mission that our Father has given to us. He has wisely allocated His gifts in the proper proportion, assuring that all are present and all needs are met.

Building "God's birdhouse"—what a glorious task we have been given! The blueprint has been presented to us—the tools are in our hands—the task is before our eyes—now all that remains is the execution, the carrying out of the mission. Somehow these words must be transformed into deeds that take place in real-life churches and communities. None are exempt, and there are no excuses. Do not say that you are too few in number and have insufficient resources to carry out all the endeavors that the building project entails. True, you may be only a handful, but there are others around you who face a similar difficulty. Why not join with them and do things together?

Maybe you feel alone, the only one who seems to be moved by the Great Commission, which is still with us. If so, then you should have empathy for the forlorn, frightened dozen or so disciples who first received that directive—and then watched their Lord disappear from their sight. There is only one difference—you are surrounded by Christians on all sides, while they were all alone. Yet the Holy Spirit empowered them to carry out a task that appeared completely impossible from a human standpoint. Do you realize that this same power is yours today, that Jesus Christ is with you every minute of the day and night, and that with Him all things are possible?

Maybe you still are looking for that assignment—the directive from your Lord that will set you moving in the right direction. Perhaps you want specific instructions, a direct command that will tell you where to place your hands. It would be presumptuous on my part to even begin to think that this book could be used to fulfill your desire. But I can share with you the markers that have served as guideposts in my journey. It might be of help to you, if you are willing to come with me on a flight of imagination.

There was a time in my life when I felt at loose ends, without a purpose, and rather worthless. It was a distressing feeling, and it left me with a downcast facial expression. One day Jesus came by and asked me to share with Him the nature of my difficulty. "Lord," I said, "I feel like there is no purpose in living. Everything seems so temporary. Nothing I do seems to satisfy my longing for meaning and fulfillment."

"Come with Me," He said, and He took me by the hand and led me into the presence of our Father. God looked at me, and then turned to Jesus and asked, "What seems to be troubling Dick?"

"He is struggling with the impression that life has lost all meaning, Father. He cannot see any purpose in his existence," was Jesus' reply.

"No purpose? No reason to be on earth?" The incredulous tone of His voice startled me. "Son," He said, "why not show him as well as tell him?"

There was an urgency in our steps as we departed, so much so that I experienced difficulty in keeping pace with my Lord. I followed Him up the steep slope of a promontory that led ever higher. We finally reached a vantage point from which we could overlook the world that lay below. For the first time I became aware of the vast masses of people that seemed to be scurrying about without a sense of direction. Some were extremely troubled, others were depressed, their empty eyes mirroring a heartrending hopelessness. What I saw tore at my emotions as my eyes filled with tears.

"Jesus," I blurted out, "what is the matter with all those people? Why aren't You out there helping them, just as You are with me. Don't You love them as much?"

I heard Him catch His breath at my remarks, and I detected a sob. Turning, I saw a face filled with anguish as tears coursed down His cheeks. His voice was choking with emotion as He said, "I do love them, every single one of them, just as much as I love you! How I wish I could help them! There is so much that I could do to end their search, to satisfy their longings."

"Then why don't You," was my thoughtless response.

He was silent for a few moments, and then He directed my attention to a lonely figure slightly to our right. "Do you see that young woman standing all by herself," He said. "Her husband was killed in an accident last week, and her heart is breaking. How I long to go to her, put My arms around her shoulders, and comfort her in her sorrow." He hesitated for a moment, looked into my eyes, and then continued, "But I have no arms—unless I have your arms."

He next pointed to a small, frightened group clustered around a carved idol, offering one sacrifice after another. "How needless that is," He cried. "How foolish of them to think that they can appease God, when I have already made the sacrifice. If only I could carry the news of their redemption to them," and again His gaze fell upon me before He finished, "but I have no feet—unless I have your feet."

We looked to our left, and there was a lonely old woman, forgotten by all those once near and dear to her, the ravages of a broken heart clearly visible on her lined features. "Oh, if only I could sit beside her and tell her that I care, that I am with her, and that she is still precious in My sight. If only I could whisper to her messages of hope, comfort, and love." His hand fell on my shoulder as He finished, "but I have no voice—unless it is your voice."

Nearby was a child afflicted with a birth defect, while alongside stood the mother and father, their struggle for understanding clearly discernible. "How I long to fill their hearts with love and compassion, to empty the contents of My heart into theirs so that they may have My peace and joy!" Now I turned to Him, and the longing was so visible and intense that my eyes overflowed. His voice fell, and in the hush I heard, "But I have no heart from which to pour—unless it is your heart."

"You are looking for a purpose, Dick," He said, "Go—go back to where you live, to your home, your job, your family, your neighborhood, your church, your world. Go back—and be My hands, My feet, My voice, and My heart!"

So I live out my life with a purpose that defies description. There is a mission, a reason for living that will be with me for as long as my heart continues to send blood coursing through my veins. It is a mission that has been given to me by a loving Father—not out of necessity on His part, for He could have chosen a more direct way to convert sinners—but because in His grace and love He has decided to use me (and you) to carry out His eternal plan of salvation. He alone is responsible for the privilege we have of being laborers together with Him. Because of this there has been injected into my life the excitement that I have always craved. It has transformed each day into an adventure, and made the night a time of peace and rest.

Isn't that what building "God's birdhouse" is all about? Isn't that why we experience an overwhelming sense of joy as we work with our Father's hand over ours? Isn't that the fulfillment of our deepest desire, the satisfying of our innermost longing?

"Go," our Lord tells us, "to those both inside and outside of My church. Go, and be My arms of comfort when there is sorrow. Go, and be My voice of hope and love to those who are lonely. Go, and be My heart so that My peace and joy can be poured into troubled lives. Go, and be My feet so that the news of My victory over Satan can be carried to the furthermost reaches of this world."

"Go," are His instructions, "and build 'My birdhouse.' "

SOLI DEO GLORIA—TO GOD BE THE GLORY